DATE DUE

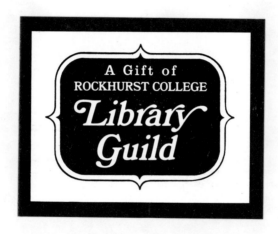

ORGANISATIONAL FUNCTIONING

Organisational Functioning

A Behavioural Analysis

MICHAEL C KNOWLES
*Monash University, Clayton,
Victoria, Australia*

Gower

Published by

Gower Publishing Company Limited.

Reprinted 1982 by Gower Publishing Company Limited, Croft Road, Aldershot, Hants, GU11 3HR, England.

British Library Cataloguing in Publication Data

Knowles, Michael
   Organisational functioning
   1 Organisational behaviour
   I Title
   301.18'32   HD58.7

ISBN 0 566 00329 5

Printed in Great Britain by Ashford Press Ltd.

Contents

Preface

This book is addressed to people who spend most of their working lives in organisations. It should be of interest to those who seek to make sense of the world in which they work and live, and to those who want to take charge of their own destinies rather than being overrun by them.

The study analysed the interrelationships between a number of dimensions of organisational behaviour. As such it dealt with problems which are as old as management itself. However, this research examined these problems from the relatively new perspective of social systems theory. By these means it was possible to integrate a variety of material in an area which to some degree has been diverse and fragmented, to offer empirical confirmation of some strongly suspected phenomena, and to identify some further properties of organisational behavior.

Since those who work in organisations and those who study organisations share a common sub-culture they both are concerned with the same questions and difficulties. The book identifies a way of organising these issues and problems so that they can be rendered more explicable and intelligible. It did this by establishing a framework within which individual occurances could be viewed as particular manifestations of a fundamental, underlying structure.

The importance of these findings for effective management of the key areas with which the study was concerned — performance, productivity, satisfaction, morale — need not be stressed. This is particularly true with respect to planning, for the results of the study signify not only that management of these areas should be elevated from a tactical to a strategic level, but also that the role played by the internal organisation in affecting these kinds of results should be fully appreciated.

Acknowledgements

I am indebted to Professor N. C. Hunt, Chairman of the Department of Business Studies at Edinburgh University, who provided the initial opportunity through the financial auspices of the Foundation for Management Education to conduct the field work in this study, and for his continued support and help during every phase of the research. I received generous co-operation from the management, employees and union officials in the company where the study was conducted, and this is deeply appreciated.

The detailed analysis of various facets of the research was carried out in my current employment at Monash University. Several journals have carried articles on individual aspects of the study and the benefit I obtained from editorial and reviewers' comments is warmly acknowledged. In particular I wish to thank Miss K. Rowe, Mr R. M. McKenzie and Professor H. Behrend of Edinburgh University; Dr R. N. Rapoport and Professor A. Clark of the Tavistock Institute of Human Relations; Professor L. Bailyn of the Massachusetts Institute of Technology; and Professor D. Cochrane, Professor A. K. Collins, Mr E. J. Vaughan and Dr P. Gilmour of Monash University.

My other sense of gratitude is towards Professor E. H. Schein and the Sloan School of Management at MIT for providing the sabbatical opportunity for writing the first draft of the current manuscript in a stimulating and invigorating environment, and the comments of Professor E. H. Schein and Professor R. H. Harris were invaluable in allowing the subsequent argument to be reshaped and refined.

My final debt is to my family, especially Ann my wife who helped as co-worker, spouse and critic; to Mr G. R. Mountain who also provided helpful suggestions on the manuscript; and to those responsible for its typing, Mrs P. M. Casey, Miss B. Golotta, Miss A. Smith and Mrs B. Chapman, and its diagrams, Mr G. R. R. Swinton and Miss S. M. Tomlins.

ORGANISATIONAL FUNCTIONING

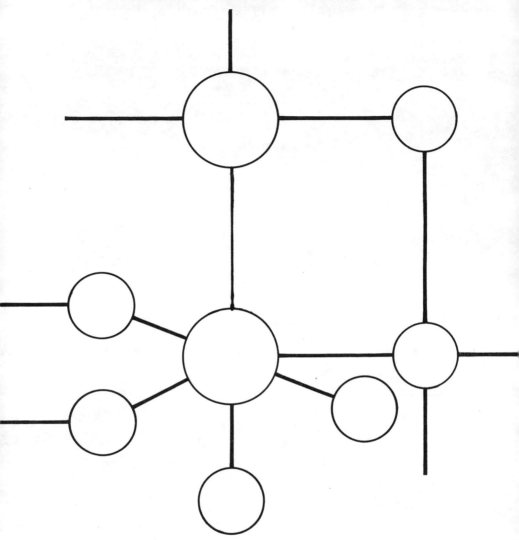

A BEHAVIOURAL ANALYSIS

1 Previous theory and research

Problems in organisation can be tantalising — both to understand and rectify. The study described here attempts to provide an empirical basis for the analysis of human behaviour in organisations, whereby it is hoped that some of its complexities will be simplified and some of its contradictions rendered more explicable. By way of introduction previous theory and research in the field are reviewed and some of the main findings and implications are discussed in this opening chapter. Subsequent chapters then outline the present research and its results in greater detail.

Introduction

Human behaviour is diverse and complex. This is one of its many charms and attractions to social scientists who try to understand how it functions and bring rhyme and reason to its variety and vicissitudes. Everyone at times is a social scientist – anyone who attempts to identify an underlying pattern so that the situation with which the person is dealing becomes more clearly understood and, therefore, easier to handle. This tendency is universal; we feel more secure and confident in managing situations if we know how and why particular events occur as they do. The only distinction is that with the social scientist the search is longer and deeper, and the explanations less tailored for a particular individual and more relevant to a wider cross-section of the community.

It is this link between knowledge and action that is increasing the significance and the importance of the social sciences to management. The logic of the connection is basic: 'Give me fish', it has been said, 'and I eat today; teach me to fish and I eat tomorrow'. The trend or development is not surprising since most managerial problems have organisational components, and thus the productive route to solving them lies in identifying the real nature of the problems more precisely. Perhaps what is surprising is that the strengthening of the behavioural basis of management has not occurred sooner.

As anybody who has worked in an organisation knows, the issues are seldom simple, often they are compound. One of the main difficulties is that it is frequently hard to come to grips with the kinds of problems that arise. We may feel we are on the right track but just when we sense we are about to reach the crux of the matter the problem becomes opaque again and disappears before our eyes like a stream vanishing into the sands of the desert. Under these conditions the practical tendency is to seek an answer to that part of the problem that can be pinned down and arrested. What is appropriate is that which suits the needs of the moment.

These kinds of solution, it can be seen, are really forms of expediency. They are helpful in the short term, but no more than this can be expected of them. One of the consequences of invoking them is that the same problem is liable to recur or, if we are especially zealous in our endeavour to contain the particular issue, it can change its mode of expression and reappear in a different guise.

3

Chameleon activity is as familiar in the social sciences as it is in the natural sciences. In fact in the social sciences real dangers can accompany this phenomenon, for a behavioural problem suppressed and driven underground can re-emerge in a fiercer and more formidable form. It can do this in the first instance by changing itself into a medium term rather than a short term problem. Similarly, long term problems can be created if our methods of diagnosis and treatment persist in being inaccurate or superficial. In this way thorny issues can be transformed into intractable problems.

It is this proposition — that lasting and long term solutions to organisational problems lie in a more searching and satisfying analysis of the issues involved — which forms the foundation for the design of the current study. The aim of the research is to take various aspects of organisational behaviour, particularly in the area of productivity and morale, performance and satisfaction, and to look for connections and linkages between the variables concerned. The intention is to move away from a level of consideration used in everyday working life and onto a plateau of analysis where more pervasive patterns of relationships may be identified. It is to be hoped that this altered interpretation of the nature of organisational issues will reveal a fresh perspective for planning practical solutions to these problems, and that this different orientation will be helpful in making the task of managing human relationships more precise, more predictable and more effective.

Established theory

In order to provide a conceptual framework within which the study would be conducted it was desirable to undertake a synopsis of the field of administrative theory. This would help in developing a frame of reference for planning the research, and would permit the results to be interpreted in an emerging and historical perspective.

Initially in the systematic study of organisations the enterprise was regarded as a legal entity where the route to efficiency lay largely in the building of optimal formal structure and the development of a system of tradition and authority to ensure that control of activities within that framework would be maintained. Two structural aspects were important — the superstructure involving outline shape, extent of centralisation or decentralisation, and design, essentially of product, process or matrix format — and an infrastructure

4

including chain of command, span of control and sub-unit size (Weber 1921, Urwick 1944, Gulick 1937, Graicunas 1937, Davis 1951, Drucker 1954, Cleland and King 1968). Constitution of the organisation along these lines was accompanied by the development of specialisation, standardisation and formalisation, creating an inevitable bureaucratic trend especially as the enterprise grew and matured (Merton 1940, Selznick 1943, Gouldner 1954, Blau 1955, Crozier 1964, Pugh, Hickson, Hinings and Turner 1968).

An alternative view of organisations arose in consequence of two observations — firstly, that the numerous activities that members engage in can vary widely from the requirements prescribed in duty statements, and secondly, that the relationships actually formed are far more complex than those designated in the organisation chart and the policies and procedures manual (Roethlisberger and Dickson 1939, Mayo 1945, Whyte 1948, Dalton 1959). This complexity arose largely out of factors that were social and psychological in nature, and brought into focus the importance of abilities, motivation, attitudes, interpersonal relations and the binding significance of leadership. At first this alternative set of activities and relationships was described as the informal organisation, and subsequently numerous structured relationships were found to exist within this sphere of behavioural activities: the organisation's role structure (Katz and Kahn 1966), its communication networks, its status structure, its power structure — all of which may be represented as overlays superimposed upon the formal authority structure (Litterer 1965).

A more recent trend has been to distinguish between structure and process. Structure refers to the formal aspects just described — to departmentalisation and stratification, line/staff relationships, tallness/flatness, and so on. Processes, on the other hand, are sequences of activities or events and arise in organisations from a variety of sources. In the first place they stem from the enterprise's various functions: operations, finance, marketing, research and development, and human resources (French 1963). For example the human resources function embraces a host of activities subsumed under such processes as employment, career development and remuneration, and the other functional areas are similarly diversified. Secondly, separate sets of processes stem from the managerial function — the need for management to co-ordinate and integrate the activities of organisational members (Fayol 1916, Barnard 1938, Follet 1942, Mooney 1947). Essentially these involve planning, reviewing and controlling. Thirdly, social processes interconnect the

5

activities of organisational members, and include communication, members' roles and functions in groups, group problem solving and decision making, group norms and group growth, leadership and authority, and intergroup co-operation and competition (Schein 1969). Lastly, there are the psychological processess such as perception, cognition, learning and motivation, and these form the final link in the chain integrating the individual and the organisation.

While both approaches contribute substantially to the understanding of organisations by virtue of their different perspectives and insights, they are essentially complementary, as illustrated in Figure 1.1. Here it is convenient to contrast the two historical developments just described: one emphasing the distinction between formal and behavioural elements, the other separating out the differences between structure and process elements. Thus, in a two-by-two sense it is possible to represent in a single model all the organisational elements encompassed by administrative theory.

Two other aspects of formal structure have been included, namely technology and size. The effect of technology upon tasks, group behaviour, social norms, job satisfaction and performance has been well investigated (Trist and Bamforth 1951, Walker and Guest 1952, Herbst 1962, and Lodahl 1964), and a number of other studies also attest to the effect of technology upon organisational form and behaviour (Woodward 1965, Harvey 1968, Hage and Aitken 1969, Hickson, Pugh and Pheysey 1969, Mahoney and Frost 1974). Similarly size is also an important structural variable, although its effect upon performance, attitudes and other behavioural characteristics may be ameliorated by many factors (Fox and Scott 1943, Acton Society Trust 1953, Revans 1958, Indik 1963).

While at this stage it is not our intention to try to unravel how these numerous factors interact we can use Figure 1.1 to incorporate some of the research dealing with sequential developments. It has been shown that the internal structure of organisations can be highly differentiated, depending upon the functions performed by its sub-units (Lawrence and Lorsch 1967). For example, a sales department operates within a dynamic market place whereas an operations department interacts with a relatively stable production technology. In each case this leads to a differentiation of processes, since members differ with respect to prior education and experience, nature of tasks performed, working style and mental processes (March and Simon 1958). In other words we can expect a differentiation in structure to be accompanied by a differentiation in processes.

Our synopsis has now enabled us to identify four major elements.

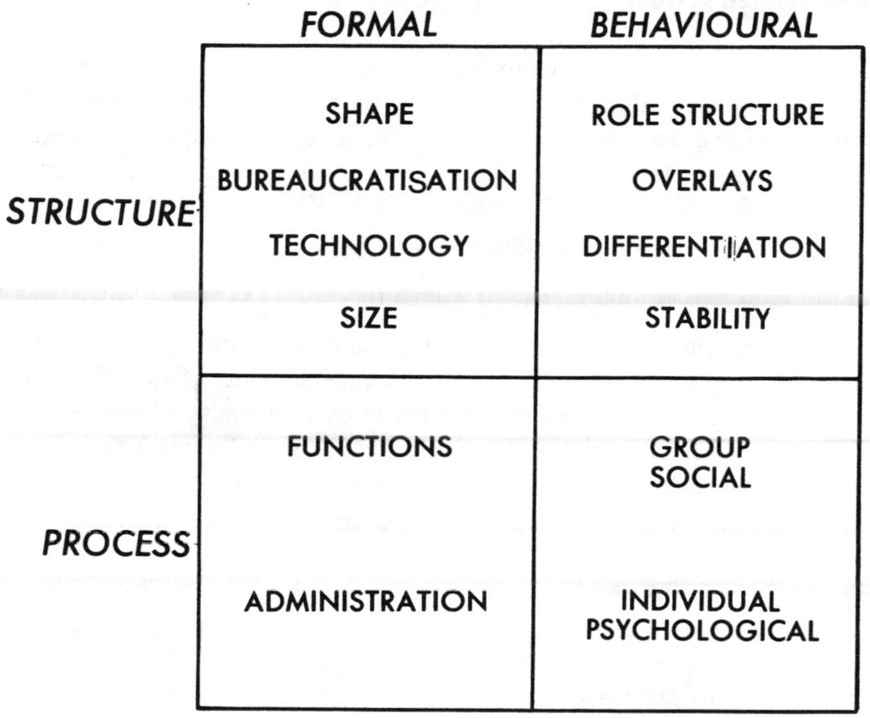

	FORMAL	BEHAVIOURAL
STRUCTURE	SHAPE BUREAUCRATISATION TECHNOLOGY SIZE	ROLE STRUCTURE OVERLAYS DIFFERENTIATION STABILITY
PROCESS	FUNCTIONS ADMINISTRATION	GROUP SOCIAL INDIVIDUAL PSYCHOLOGICAL

Figure 1.1 Anatomy of the organisation as seen from different perspectives in adminstrative theory.

or sets of activites and these form the cornerstones upon which administrative theory rests. They are shown in simplified form in Figure 1.2 which serves at this point to consolidate our selective overview of a wide ranging and diverse literature.

An integrated system

Although it is helpful to examine the anatomy of organisations in the way just described it still remains to represent the totality of their activities, and systems theory has been developed to meet this need (von Bertalanffy 1950, 1956, Miller 1955, Haire 1959, Ackoff 1960, Simon 1962, Schein 1965, Katz and Kahn 1966). Here the organisation-environment matrix has been illustrated in Figure 1.3.

In this figure S_{oo} refers to the innumerable activities within the organisation, the large number of social and technical relationships, and the sentiments arising out of the interactions. S_{ee} refers to enviromental influences and is constituted by a diversity of elements, economic, political, social and technical; and S_{oe}, S_{eo} refer to interactions between the organisation and its environment.

The advent of systems theory was a major development in the field since it took the total organisation as the unit of analysis and brought into focus the interaction between the sub-systems within the organisation. For example the research of Trist, Higgin, Murray and Pollock (1963) in particular demonstrated the repercussions that a technical sub-system could effect upon the social organisation of work, and illustrated the need for corporate policy to develop the potential in both sub-systems concurrently so that the capacity of the total system could be optimised. Subsequent research has sought ways of balancing both technical requirements and human needs, and the composite work organisation described by Trist et al. provided a good example of this kind of optimising solution.

The other advantage of sytems theory was that emphasis swung from internal relationships to the external environment in which the organisation functioned, e.g. Burns and Stalker (1961), Rice (1963) and Lawrence and Lorsch (1967). Whether an organisation is located in a static or turbulent field has important implications for its structure, the managerial processes that develop, and the kinds of internal relationships and attitudes that are established (Emery and

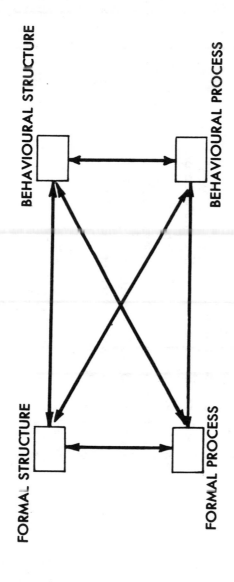

Figure 1.2 Elements within organisations

Note: Lines represent interactions between elements; arrows represent reciprocal relationships.

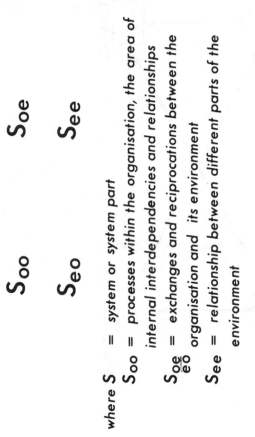

where S = system or system part

S_{oo} = processes within the organisation, the area of internal interdependencies and relationships

$S_{oe/eo}$ = exchanges and reciprocations between the organisation and its environment

S_{ee} = relationship between different parts of the environment

Figure 1.3 The organisation–environment constituting one total system.

Trist 1963). Effective organisations are those which successfully monitor environmental changes and are able to implement appropriate alternations in organisational structure and process, or more specially have the managerial resources to institutionalise an adaptive coping cycle of activities (Schein 1965).

By virtue of these advances Figure 1.2 may be elaborated to incorporate these relationships, as shown in Figure 1.4.

Figure 1.4 has been developed to show the environmental impact of economic , political, social and technical factors upon structures and processes, and to indicate the key role of top management in anticipating and synthesising these effects by identifying and specifying the organisation's formal goals and formulating an imaginative corporate policy which will ensure that strategic objectives will be attained.

Relevance of previous research

Although systems theory has provided an integrating theoretical model few studies have come to terms with analysing the functioning of organisations as total systems. Two studies stand out as exceptions in this regard.

Mechanistic and organic organisations

One of the first studies of its kind in this area was conducted by Burns and Stalker (1961) who drew attention to two fundamentally different kinds of organisations operating in the electronics industry − the mechanistic and the organic. With the mechanistic organisation problems and tasks were broken down into specialisms, and technical methods, duties and powers pertaining to each position tended to be precisely defined. Operations and working behaviour of members were governed by decisions made and instructions issued by superiors, which tended to result in the development of interpersonal interactions that were vertical in nature. Communication patterns also tended to be vertically oriented with amplification of downward communication and filtering of upward communication. These kinds of systems were most appropriate to enterprises operating under relatively stable conditions.

In organic organisations problems and tasks were not so thoroughly broken down and allotted to specialist postions, and the organisational hierarchy was not so clearly defined. Methods, duties and powers were influenced by interactions between people, and

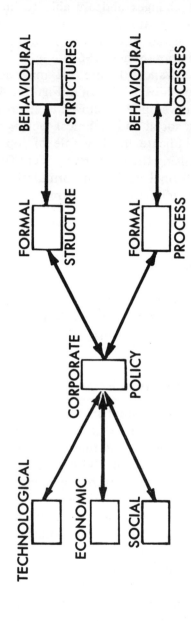

Figure 1.4 Elements within organisation—environment matrix

Note: Lines represent primary relationships; secondary relationships not shown

these interactions ran laterally as much as vertically. Communication was comparable to lateral consultation rather than vertical command. These systems were more adaptive to unstable conditions characterised by more rapidly changing environments.

Conventional and composite work organisations

Subsequent research by Trist et al. (1963) again took a global veiw of the organisation of work, this time in the Durham coalfields. With the advent of new, sophisticated machinery the jobs of the miners and the traditional reliance upon teamwork were fundamentally altered. The new jobs tended to be simple and repetitive on account of the higher degree of specialisation, which also meant that there were fewer opportunities in which the miners could cooperate when difficulties arose on particular shifts. Not only was the new work organisation more inflexible, but inability to help each other physically meant that the miners could not support and assist each other psychologically, a particularly important factor for them given the dangerous nature of the work they were doing. This was called the conventional work organisation.

Under parallel conditions with identical technical characteristics as far as machinery and equipment were concerned the work was organised along different lines so that the miners were trained over a wider range of tasks. They were able to rotate jobs within shifts and between shifts according to work needs. More responsibility was delegated to shifts, particularly for planning the operations, allocating individuals to jobs, and training, so that the shifts were self-sufficient in terms of mining skill. This was described as the composite work organisation.

It is useful to compare the results of the two types of organisation. The composite came out better on all indexes — there was lower absence, lower labour turnover and a lower incidence of neurotic illness among the miners. Productivity, measured as output per man-shift, was 5.3 tons for the latter as compared with 3.5 tons for the former.

Summary

This overview of the literature has served to identify the major elements determining organisational functioning (Figure 1.4). It has been shown that systems theory offers a fruitful way for enabling this complex set of elements to be conceived as an entity. The research of Burns and Stalker and Trist et al. has provided pioneering attempts to represent the organisation or sub-organisation as a totality, with the Trist study drawing explicity upon systems theory as its source of inspiration.

2   The research programme

This chapter outlines the aims of the study and then describes the research design by which the purpose of the investigation could be fulfilled, including an account of the location of the research, the sample used, the method of assessment employed, and a discussion of the initial results.

Previous research has attempted to identify the kinds of variables occurring within Figure 1.4, and in a causal sense to establish the effects of these elements upon other kinds of variables involving or connected with productivity and morale, or performance and satisfaction. Particular studies have examined, for example, the effect of different supervisory methods on productivity, absenteeism and labour turnover (Argyle, Gardner and Cioffi 1958), the influence of different patterns of leadership on grievances and labour turnover (Fleishman and Harris 1962), the use of teamwork to reduce labour turnover (Mayo and Lombard 1944), and the impact of assembly line organisation on output, quality and morale (Van Beck 1964). This trend has probably been exemplified most clearly in the work of Likert (1967), who distinguished between causal, intervening and end-result variables, as shown in Figure 2.1.

Similar developments have occurred in systems theory, where the relationships between the elements internal to an organisation and the system output variables have been represented in Figure 2.2, adapted from Cooper and Foster (1971).

All this work has tended to give us one view of how organisations function. Is there a different approach? And if so will the answers it provides be essentially different? To obtain a lead on these kinds of questions it was helpful to turn to the research of Herbst (1957) who has advocated an alternative method of studying the internal structure of an organisation without altering its internal functioning: the manner by which a system transforms a given set of inputs into outputs may be examined, and from the input—output relationship the internal structure may be inferred. Herbst used his method to examine the sales data of British retail establishments and to relate changes in their administrative structure to changes in their volume of sales.

In so far as system output data were utilised, the method developed in the present research was similar to the approach used by Herbst. The main point of departure, however, lay in the idea of examing the interrelationship between the system output variables, and from these results to infer the nature of internal structure. In terms of Figure 2.3 the aim was to focus upon how a system (organisation or sub-organisation) functioned in an organic sense, and to designate a more comprehensive range of criterion variables than used in previous research in the anticipation that this would more

Causal variables	Intervening variables	End result variables
interpersonal relationships	attitudes between peers and towards superior	production
group processes	communication	quality
		absence
type of leadership	nature of goals w.r.t. output quality	labour turnover

Figure 2.1 Simplified format for representing relationships between organisational variables.

Work Relationship Structure		System Outputs
Human Inputs	Technical Characteristics	
individual performance	level of mechanization	performance
psychological requirements	technological layout	satisfaction
social interaction	nature of processed material	stability

Figure 2.2 An input—conversion—output model of a socio-technical system.

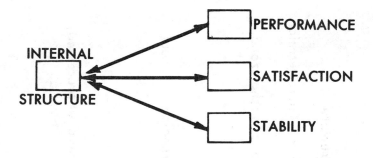

Figure 2.3 Suggested relationship between internal structure and performance satisfaction and stability.

likely reveal essentail structure within the system should it exist in any shape or form. In other words by working back from performance, satisfaction and stability, as shown in Figure 2.3, the aim was to determine what kind of picture would emerge when a fundamentally different type of research design and method of analysis was employed.

Choice of unit of analysis

There would have been many attractions in choosing a number of organisations and assessing these with respect to selected criterion variables. This, however, would have created a host of methodological problems, for if systematic differences were found between the organisations these results could be attributed to any of the large number of variables known to affect work and organisational behaviour.

Technology may be cited as one major variable affecting group and individual behaviour, so if the organisations were drawn from separate industries or even from the same industry, it would have been difficult, and certainly costly, to have picked a sample guaranteeing that plant layout and design were comparable in all cases. Similar arguments can be advanced regarding size, nature of market served by the organisations, and economic conditions affecting the industries.

The strategy developed to circumvent these problems was to conduct an intraorganisational study in which sub-units of the organisation became the units of analysis. The primary intention was that it would be easier to equate sub-units within the same organisation on the external variables just described than it would be to equate total organisations with respect to these factors. While this meant moving from a higher order to a lower order system it was hoped that any loss in attraction would be outweighed by advantages deriving from precision and comparability.

Choice of criterion variables

Compared with previous organisational studies the aim was to broaden substantially the range of system outputs. Clearly many variables characterise organisational behaviour, so in this case choice was restricted to the kind of criterion variables which would represent how adequately the system functioned. Variables were selected to encompass performance, satisfaction and stability. Within these three broad areas specific variables were respectively identified: production, quality, and costs; job satisfaction of employees, job satisfaction of supervisors, and work anxiety; accidents, absence, labour turnover, and industrial unrest.

This list was not selected in any definitive sense — the idea was merely that this set would cover comprehensively but not necessarily exhaustively the more important manifestations of work and organisational behaviour.

The matrix representing the basic design of the study is shown in Table 2.1.

Summary

The plan of the study may now be summarised: it was to choose a number of organisational units which operated under similar technological and environmental conditions, and to assess each with respect to a range of system outputs. It was thought that any substantive differences between the organisational units would be portrayed by the criterion variables, and from the interrelationships so obtained aspects of internal structure distinguishing the units should be identified.

From the results obtained with the organisational units it may be possible tentatively to generalise the results to total organisation, although subsequent research would be necessary to test the validity of these further expectations.

Location

In conducting the study 14 organisational units or sections were chosen which comprised a single division of a light engineering company. There were 12 manufacturing sections, designated 'a' to 'l' and two assembly sections, designated 'm' and 'n'. Work in all sections was light and repetitive, both men and women were employed, and no distinction was made between the sections in terms of the company's selection and placement policies. These conditions made for technical comparability of the organisational units, and since all sections came under the authority of the one divisional manager, structure and process effects emanating from top management were also generally equivalent. Furthermore, economic activity was stable over the period of the study, and under these external conditions demand for the division's product was

Table 2.1

Assessment of different work situations on ten organisational variables

	Organisational variables									
Cases	P	Q	C	JSE	JSS	WA	Ac	Ab	LT	IU
1										
.										
.										
.										
n										

P	= production	WA	=	work anxiety
Q	= quality	Ac	=	accidents
C	= costs	Ab	=	absence
JSE	= job satisfaction of employees	LT	=	labour turnover
JSS	= job satisfaction of supervisors	IU	=	industrial unrest

steady and affected all sections alike.

The study was conducted in Scotland, in a city located in the industrial region of the country. With regard to the policies and practices of the company, especially as far as the management of human resources was concerned, the company was like many in the field, neither behind the times nor in advance of them.

Sample

The division employed approximately 314 employees (Appendix 1). No personal data were collected from these employees, apart from the identification of the sections in which they worked. It was thought that the collecting of biographical information may deter some from completing the job satisfaction questionnaire, for if data other than section of employment were asked for it might appear possible that individual questionnaires could be identified. Since the personal data were not essential for the purposes of the study they were forsaken in order to maximise the questionnaire response rate.

Also no attempt was made to balance the sections according to age, length of service, marital status, or similar variables. It was assumed that with an employment strength of this size variables such as these would be randomly distributed throughout the divison, and certainly no visible clustering of any effect was noticeable either to management or the researcher.

Measurement

Company records were used as the primary source of information and provided the basic data for all the variables, with the exception of production, job satisfaction and work anxiety. With respect to these variables production was assessed by means of a rating scale, and job satisfaction and work anxiety were assessed by a question-naire used in previous research. It was not an objective of the present study to undertake fundamental research in the field of measurement. Rather, existing techniques were employed with a view to analysing the nature of the resulting data.

In all instances except when the questionnaire was used assessment was made over a period of six months so as to ensure general stability of the measures. Apart from this period it took approximately a further eighteen months to gather all the data and prepare them for initial analysis. During this time the researcher became well acquainted with the members of division and the work in which they were engaged. This experience was invaluable when it came to interpreting the significance of the results.[1]

Production

Although the requirement that the shop order be met was so clearly important to the division, this proved to be one of the most difficult criteria on which to compare the performance of the sections, since the weekly achievement of the shop order was recorded for the division as a whole but not for the individual sections.

A second objective index of performance that was considered was the standard labour costs, for this would have given a measure of the actual production achieved by the sections. It was thought that differences between the actual and the budgeted figure could be compared, but again the weekly budgeted figure could not be determined for the individual sections.

Because of the difficulties in obtaining a method of comparison based on company records a rating method was used. Within the company's organisation the co-ordination of the sections' production was the responsibility of the materials' controller. The materials' controller and his two assistants were instructed in making a composite ranking of the sections on their ability to meet the weekly shop order over the six month period. These three people were specifically directed to consider production records only in establishing the ranking, which is shown in Table 2.2.

Table 2.2

Ranking of all sections on production achievement over the six month period

	Section													
	a	b	c	d	e	f	g	h	i	j	k	l	m	n
Ranking	1.5	4	14	7.5	10.5	5	1.5	9	3	6	13	12	10.5	7.5

Note: Half scores used to indicate tied ranks.

B Quality

As with production, some difficulty was encountered in assessing the quality performance of the sections. Sampling inspection was carried out for the entire division, but this was primarily a managerial control to prevent inferior work from going through, and the information was not kept as a record of quality performance. The costs incurred through scrap and repairs, however, were tabulated as part of the weekly expenditures of each section, and these figures were therefore used as the basis for assessment. As the sections differed in size the absolute expenditure figures could not be taken for purposes of comparison, but this difficulty was overcome by calculating the total expenditures on scrap and repairs and comparing these with the budgeted expenditures. The quality performance of each section was then assessed according to the extent to which it achieved, or failed to achieve, its scrap and repair targets.

The performance of each section calculated in this way is shown in Table 2.3. A negative sign indicates performance within the budget.

Table 2.3

Differences between budget and actual scrap and repair costs for each section over the six month period

Differences between budgeted and actual costs (percentages)	a	b	c	d	e	f	g	h	i	j	k	l	m	n
	−6.4	−10.7	−2.2	4.3	17.5	9.0	−2.3	8.2	11.0	−7.7	−25.5	2.9	−10.1	−2.6

Note: A negative sign indicates performance within the budget.

Costs

Since sales were completely outside the control of the division, manufacturing costs were of major importance as they formed the division's primary contribution to the company's profitability. The difference between the standard costs of manufacture and the actual costs was particularly important, for identification of these variances enabled control action to be taken at the operational level, so it was in this direction that the method of assessing the cost performance of the sections was developed.

Although standard costing involves major elements such as materials, labour and overheads (Henrici 1960), the costing system of this company gave more emphasis to labour costs as these were the most variable ones. A weekly labour expenditure report was pre-

26

pared by the cost controller of the division to facilitate cost control. Since this information was used as the basis for assessing the cost performance of the sections, the weekly expenditure report, and the way it was compiled, are described in Appendix 2.

A measure of cost effectiveness was needed that reflected each section's ability to contain its cost of manufacture. As Horngren (1967) stated this may be indicated not so much by the absolute costs incurred but by a unit's capability to work towards and achieve its budgeted costs. The difference, then, between budgeted costs and actual costs was taken as the measure of cost effectiveness.

The annual budget was available for each section, and the overall target for cost performance was obtained by expressing the sum of direct labour losses, hourly paid indirect labour, and overtime and nightshift as a percentage of direct labour. This served to relate expenses for non-productive labour to those for productive labour.[2]

Cost performance was recorded over the six months and the differences between the budgeted percentages and the actual percentages are shown in Table 2.4 below. In this table the positive signs indicate expenditures in excess of budget.

Table 2.4

Differences between budgeted costs and actual costs for each section
over the six month period

Differences between budgeted and actual costs (percentages)	Section													
	a	b	c	d	e	f	g	h	i	j	k	l	m	n
	−41.0	25.6	10.5	3.9·	7.2	50.8	−6.5	5.0	44.2	−27.4	4.2	−2.5	−5.0	36.6

Note: Positive signs indicate expenditures in excess of budget.

Job satisfaction of employees

Job satisfaction can be assessed in many ways but for this study the interpretation of Walker and Lumsden (1963) was used, where job satisfaction was considered to be a complex product of a person's satisfaction with particular aspects of his job. Hence satisfaction on each of a number of specific aspects could be measured first of all, and from these results overall job satisfaction could be computed.

Job satisfaction was assessed in this study by means of a questionnaire which covered ten different job aspects. These were: communication, company and management, physical working conditions, security, social, supervision, wages, work ease, work interest and work

27

variety. Each job aspect has been defined in Table 2.5. The questionnaire, used previously by Mountain (1965), covered those job aspects which past research had shown to be important to factory employees. Items used in the questionnaire were selected so that the correlations with the job aspect to which they referred were high, and were low with any other job aspect.

Administration: Support for conducting the survey was obtained from management, and also from the union representing the shop floor employees in the division. Shop floor representatives from the 14 sections were nominated by both supervisors and trade union shop stewards; a lunch-hour meeting of the shop floor representatives was held in which the nature of the questionnaire and the type of questions were described to them; and they were asked if they would distribute and collect the questionnaires. It was stressed that the questionnaires were to be completed anonymously, and the results would be confidentail. The response rate was 66 per cent.

Scoring: In completing the questionnaire respondents placed a cross on a five point scale to indicate their agreement or disagreement with a given statement. These were scored from zero to four, with the higher score indicating greater satisfaction. With four questions for each job aspect, the possible range of scores for each was 0-16.

Preliminary results: The level of satisfaction on each job aspect was assessed for all the employees in the division, and average levels of satisfaction were then obtained for each of the 14 sections. These results are shown in Table 2.6.

In order to examine differences between the sections, each was ranked according to its average satisfaction score on all the job aspects. These rankings are shown in Table 2.7 where the sections have been rearranged according to their overall rankings.

Table 2.7 shows that the sections ranged from ones such as 'n', 'c' and 'j' with relatively high levels of job satisfaction to those such as 'f', 'i' and 'l' which were characterised by low levels of satisfaction. The tendency for individual sections to have similar rankings on the job aspects was tested statistically and found to be highly significant (with Friedman's Two-way Analysis of Variance by Ranks, $X^2 = 57.11, p < 0.001$).

Because of the significant differences found in the levels of satisfaction between the sections, an overall ranking was obtained, as

Table 2.5

Description of each of the ten job aspects

Aspects of the Job	Description
Communication (Com)	Knowing what is happening, and what is going to happen within the work place
Company and Management (C & M)	Includes what the employee thinks of the company, and what he thinks is the management's feeling towards him
Physical Working Conditions (PWC)	Physical aspects of the work place which are not a part of the work
Security (Se)	The feeling that the employee's job will go on either with the present company, or in the same type of work
Social Aspects of the Job (So)	Feelings of employees towards other employees, particularly their workmates
Supervision (Su)	Feelings of employees towards their supervisors
Wages (W)	The total amount of pay
Work Ease (WE)	Easiness of the job
Work Interest (WI)	Interest in the job, and sense of pride in doing the work
Work Variety (WV)	The number of different things to do in the job

Table 2.6

Assessment of all sections on the job aspects

Section	Com	C & M	PWC	Se	So	Su	W	WE	WI	WV
a	7.0	4.3	7.0	5.8	11.0	11.0	6.5	5.5	9.0	9.3
b	5.0	6.5	6.7	6.6	7.5	6.4	5.4	8.2	9.7	7.7
c	6.7	6.9	9.8	9.2	8.0	8.7	7.4	9.2	10.9	7.7
d	6.6	6.3	7.7	6.8	7.9	6.8	6.0	8.0	9.9	8.1
e	4.6	6.3	8.2	6.5	5.2	6.7	6.3	10.5	9.3	8.1
f	4.6	6.4	4.7	6.9	8.0	6.3	4.6	7.7	9.6	7.3
g	4.8	5.5	8.1	9.2	7.6	6.8	6.7	7.0	10.9	9.0
h	7.6	5.5	6.9	6.4	11.8	8.0	7.1	10.4	10.4	9.4
i	4.0	5.8	5.7	5.8	7.8	5.2	5.2	8.3	9.3	6.9
j	6.6	7.1	10.7	8.2	8.2	6.3	7.3	10.7	9.4	10.0
k	4.9	6.6	6.6	6.4	7.9	8.0	5.4	8.6	9.4	4.8
l	4.0	4.4	4.8	4.1	4.9	5.4	4.5	9.3	6.9	4.4
m	5.0	5.9	6.9	6.5	9.3	6.2	4.6	10.3	11.2	8.0
n	7.1	6.7	7.7	9.1	10.0	7.9	7.4	9.4	12.7	8.3

Com   = communication

C & M = company and management

PWC   = physical working conditions

Se   = security

So   = social

Su = supervision

W   = wages

WE = work ease

WI = work interest

WV = work variety

Table 2.7

Ranked satisfaction on each job aspect for each section

Job Aspect	Section													
	n	c	j	h	g	d	a	m	e	b	k	f	i	1
Com	2	4	5.5	1	10	5.5	3	7.5	11.5	7.5	9	11.5	13.5	13.5
C & M	3	2	1	11.5	11.5	7.5	14	9	7.5	5	4	6	10	13
PWC	5.5	2	1	8.5	4	5.5	7	8.5	3	10	11	14	12	13
Se	3	1.5	4	10.5	1.5	6	12.5	8.5	8.5	7	10.5	5	12.5	14
So	3	6.5	5	1	11	8.5	2	4	13	12	8.5	6.5	10	14
Su	3	2	10.5	3.5	6.5	6.5	1	12	8	9	3.5	10.5	14	13
W	1.5	1.5	3	4	5	8	6	12.5	7	9.5	9.5	12.5	11	14
WE	5	7	1	3	13	11	14	4	2	10	8	12	9	6
WI	1	3.5	9.5	5	3.5	6	13	2	11.5	7	9.5	8	11.5	14
WV	5	9.5	1	2	4	6.5	3	8	6.5	9.5	13	11	12	14
Sum of Ranks	32	39.5	41.5	50	70	71	75.5	76	78.5	86.5	86.5	97	115.5	128.5

Job satisfaction of supervisors

A job satsifaction questionnaire similar to that used for the employees was administered to the 14 supervisors in charge of the sections constituting the division. Slight modifications were made to some of the job aspects, and the new description is shown in Appendix 3. Responses were also scored by the same method as in the previous questionnaire.

Preliminary results: The level of satisfaction on each job aspect was obtained for each supervisor. These scale scores are shown in Table 2.8.

In order that differences between the supervisors could be highlighted the data pertaining to each job aspect were ranked, as shown in Table 2.9 where the sections have been rearranged according to their overall ranking.

It can be seen from Table 2.9 that supervisors tended to be consistent in their attitudes towards the job aspects, so that supervisor 'k' for example tended to be relatively satisfied with most job aspects, in contrast with supervisor 'c' who was generally dissatisfied with these job aspects. This pattern of results was tested statistically and found to be significant (with Friedman's Two-Way Analysis of Variance by Ranks, X^2 = 24.23, p<0.05).

Because of the significant differences in the levels of satisfaction between the supervisors an overall ranking was obtained, as shown in Table 2.9.

Work anxiety

While the contribution of work to satisfaction has been well researched (over 4,000 articles according to Bordow 1974), far less has been done by way of examining the work situation as a source of pressure and conflict.

In the present study it was expected that if differences occurred between the sections on the other variables, some sections may also be more stressful to work in than others, in which case the incidence of psychosomatic symptoms would vary between the sections.

In order that this supposition could be tested the job satisfaction questionnaire was constructed to contain four questions pertaining to occupational health, and covered aspects such as tiredness, head-

Table 2.8

Assessment for all supervisors on the job aspects

Section	Com	Coy	PWC	Se	So	Mgt	W	WE	WI	WV
a	4	6	12	8	12	14	2	4	16	4
b	2	6	8	12	13	7	7	8	9	6
c	4	3	3	4	9	8	0	4	12	12
d	5	4	6	5	10	10	1	4	13	12
e	4	5	10	2	6	5	1	8	12	10
f	9	5	7	12	10	8	2	5	16	9
g	8	8	14	7	5	12	14	4	14	11
h	10	8	6	10	16	12	0	2	14	2
i	7	9	5	8	11	7	2	2	10	15
j	5	5	14	8	12	15	10	1	12	12
k	8	9	11	12	13	11	4	6	13	12
l	10	5	6	12	10	6	0	0	10	8
m	8	5	9	7	15	12	3	4	16	8
n	8	8	12	8	16	8	0	8	12	12

Table 2.9

Ranked satisfaction on each job aspect for all supervisors

Job aspect	Section													
	k	n	g	j	m	f	a	h	b	i	d	l	e	c
Com	5.5	5.5	5.5	9.5	5.5	3	12	1.5	14	8	9.5	1.5	12	12
Coy	1.5	4	4	10	10	10	6.5	4	6.5	1.5	13	10	10	14
PWC	5	3.5	1.5	1.5	7	9	3.5	11	8	13	11	11	6	14
Se	2.5	7.5	10.5	7.5	10.5	2.5	7.5	5	2.5	7.5	12	2.5	14	13
So	4.5	1.5	14	6.5	3	10	6.5	1.5	4.5	8	10	10	13	12
Mgt	6	9	4	1	4	9	2	4	11.5	11.5	7	13	14	9
W	4	12.5	1	2	5	7	7	12.5	3	7	9.5	12.5	9.5	12.5
WE	4	2	8	13	8	5	8	11.5	2	11.5	8	14	2	8
WI	6.5	9.5	4.5	9.5	2	2	2	4.5	14	12.5	6.5	12.5	9.5	9.5
WV	4	4	7	4	10.5	9	13	14	12	1	4	10.5	8	4
Sum or ranks	43.5	59	60	64.5	65.5	66.5	68	69.5	78	81.5	90.5	97.5	98	108

aches and eyestrain. These were scored in a similar way to the job satisfaction items, and again total scores could range from 0 to 16. Responses were scored so that a high score indicated the presence of work anxiety.

Preliminary results: Anxiety scores for all employees in each section were averaged and these scale scores are shown in Table 2.10.

Table 2.10
Levels of work anxiety prevailing in all sections

Level of work anxiety	Section													
	a	b	c	d	e	f	g	h	i	j	k	l	m	n
	6.0	5.9	5.3	7.0	5.2	7.8	4.7	4.7	5.6	2.4	6.9	7.5	5.4	2.7

Note: A high score indicates the presence of work anxiety.

Accidents

It is possible to define an accident in a number of different ways, and the corresponding measures used in each case may greatly affect the incidence of accidents found in any one factory. On the one hand an accident may be said to occur every time an injury is sustained, while on the other hand it may be held that an accident should be counted only if the magnitude of the injury is such that work is appreciably interrupted.

A further consideration is that accidents are difficult to measure accurately. As Hill and Trist (1953) suggested, there are wide differences between people's readiness to report accidents, with some people reporting even slight mishaps, and others seeking medical attention only for the severest of injuries. Furthermore,as the present study showed, the readiness of people to record accidents varied considerably. Over some periods both minor and major accidents were entered in the accident log book while at other times only the latter were recorded.

The most accurate measure available was considered to be the frequency of legally reportable accidents, involving the loss of three or more working shifts. On this basis the average frequency per employee of reportable lost-time accidents for each section was calculated and is shown in Table 2.11.[3]

Table 2.11

Average frequency per employee of reportable lost-time accidents
for each section over the six month period

a	b	c	d	e	f	g	h	i	j	k	l	m	n
–	0.03	–	–	0.11	–	–	–	0.04	–	0.07	–	–	–

Absence

As has been established many factors may cause people to be absent
from work (Gaudet 1957). Apart from self-evident influences such
as sickness, absence rates tend to vary according to different personal characteristics,[4] changes in economic activity, [5] and certain
job conditions.[6]

Probably because absence can be influenced by such a diversity of
factors there has always been some difficulty in finding ways to
measure it. For example, Kerr (1950) and Kerr, Koppelmeier and
Sullivan (1951) suggested that the different types of absenteeism,
excused, unexcused and total, were all unrelated, and accordingly
took separate measures of each. Alternatively, Huse and Taylor
(1962) calculated frequency as well as severity. Their measures
were: absence severity (total number of days absent), absence
frequency (total number of times absent), attitudinal absence (frequency of one-day absences, assuming that the employee did not
want to come to work), and medical absence (frequency of absences
of three days or longer, assuming that the employee was unable to
come to work). In the Kerr studies it was found that excused
absence was unrelated to unexcused absence. The Huse and Talor
study was conducted over a two year period, and found that with
absence frequency and attitudinal absences the levels were similar in
both years, but with absence severity and medical absence the rates
in successive years bore no relationship to one another.

Because of this evidence that different measures of absence
reflected different kinds of absence behaviour, four methods of
assessment were taken in the present study. Initially, absence was
measured according to whether or not it was taken with a doctor's

36

certificate. Then, both severity and frequency measures were recorded within the certificated and uncertificated absence categories. Severity was measured by the duration of time that a person was absent from his place of work over a six month period; frequency was measured as the number of spearate absence events occurring during this same period of time.

Preliminary results: The average number of times employees in the division were absent from work over the six month period was 11.8, involving a total of 62.5 hours. A breakdown of the rates, averaged for each of the 14 sections within the division according to section size, is shown in Table 2.12.

From Table 2.12 it will be observed that there was a wide range in the levels of absence between the sections. For example, certificated absence in Section 'k' was over seven times as high as in section 'j', and with uncertificated absence Section 'i' had over eleven times the rate of section 'a'.

In order to see whether the sections affected by certificated absence were also affected by uncertificated absence, and whether the sections high in absence frequency were also high in absence severity, the 14 sections were ranked on these different absence measures, as shown in Table 2.13.

Table 2.13 shows that some sections tended to have generally low rankings, while other sections generally had high rankings. This tendency was found to be statistically significant (with Kendall's coefficient of concordance, $W = 0.48$, $p < 0.05$). Because of the consistency in absence measures within sections an overall ranking of the sections was obtained, as shown in Table 2.13.

Labour turnover

Like absenteeism, but perhaps even more so, labour turnover may be related to innumerable factors, as reviews of the literature reveal (e.g. Knowles 1964, Pettman 1973, Porter and Steers 1973). Although this research has shown that well over 50 variables could be associated with labour turnover, four influences stand out as being predominant, namely the level of economic activity,[7] certain personal characteristics,[8] job and job related characteristics,[9] and organisational factors.[10]

Table 2.12

Absence rates for each of the 14 sections

Type of absence	a	b	c	d	e	f	g	h	i	j	k	l	m	n	Range
Certificated															
Severity (hours)	24.0	23.4	45.2	28.9	19.8	38.7	19.0	39.3	40.0	9.0	64.0	25.0	42.6	19.2	9.0–64.0
Frequency (times)	0.5	0.8	0.7	0.9	0.4	0.6	0.7	1.5	1.0	0.4	1.0	0.7	1.1	0.5	0.4– 1.5
Uncertificated															
Severity (hours)	4.2	34.6	26.0	21.2	19.2	27.0	18.4	35.9	49.8	27.7	22.4	46.9	19.8	33.5	4.2–49.8
Frequency (times)	5.8	10.4	10.2	7.7	8.1	5.8	12.2	9.8	17.5	10.3	9.3	13.5	10.3	7.7	5.8–17.5

Table 2.13

Ranking of the 14 sections on the different absence measures

Type of absence	Section													
	a	e	n	j	g	f	d	c	b	k	m	l	h	i
Certificated														
Severity (hours)	6	4	3	1	2	9	8	13	5	14	12	7	10	11
Frequency (times)	3.5	1.5	3.5	1.5	7	5	10	7	9	11.5	13	7	14	11.5
Uncertificated														
Severity (hours)	1	3	10	9	2	8	5	7	11	6	4	13	12	14
Frequency (times)	1.5	5	3.5	9.5	12	1.5	3.5	8	11	6	9.5	13	7	14
Sum of ranks	12	13.5	20	21	23	23.5	26.5	35	36	37.5	38.5	40	43	50.5

Measurement: Because all 14 sections were subject to the same external economic conditions, since there was no difference between the sections regarding the company's employment and placement policies, and as work in all sections was similar in nature, labour turnover could be measured in the straightforward and traditional way by expressing the number of leavers as a percentage of the average employment over the period.

i.e. $$LT = \frac{n}{\frac{N_1 + N_2}{2}} \times 100\%$$

where n = number of leavers over the period
N_1 = number of employees at beginning of period
N_2 = number of employees at end of period.

The labour turnover rate for the whole division over the period was 29.4 per cent. The rates for each section are shown in Table 2.14.

Table 2.14

Labour turnover rates for all sections over the six month period

Labour turnover	Section													
	a	b	c	d	e	f	g	h	i	j	k	l	m	n
%	16.7	27.6	31.8	8.0	15.8	38.1	4.4	19.0	52.7	21.7	27.6	45.0	36.0	0.0

Industrial unrest

It has been suggested by Whyte (1956) that the written grievance is not a good indicator of the state of affairs on the shop floor. To support this proposition he cited Roy's (1954) study in which few grievances were processed although the employees were hostile towards management. This hostility was worked out through restriction of production. Also, Dalton (1959) found that many of the dealings between unions and management over what would normally be considered to be grievances were seldom formalised as written grievances.

Although the absence of a grievance may not indicate good industrial relations, Whyte also suggested that, in general, the presence of processed grievances does indicate widespread employee discontent, so with the previous limitations in mind the number of 'failures-to-agree' was considered to be a useful objective index in reflecting the state of industrial unrest within the sections.

A grievance is a complaint by an employee against a company for an alleged transgression of his rights, as defined by the employment contract or by precedent. The grievance process aims to assess the complaint and if it is valid to have the violation corrected. In the company a failure-to-agree was registered when a grievance that an employee raised with his supervisor was forwarded to the shop steward, and agreement could not be reached between the shop steward and the supervisor. At this stage the industrial relations officer became involved in the process of conciliation, and each event of this kind was recorded by the company in a log book.

From the company log book the frequency of failures-to-agree was obtained for each section over the period of the study. These frequencies are shown in Table 2.15.[11]

Table 2.15

Frequency of failures-to-agree for each section over the six month period

	Section													
Failure to agree (frequency)	a	b	c	d	e	f	g	h	i	j	k	l	m	n
	—	—	—	—	—	1	—	—	5	—	—	—	—	—

Initial results

Differences between sections

In formulating the design of the study there were two initial expectations: that interrelationships between the variables and differences between the sections could be systematically examined. To facilitate both kinds of analyses the data obtained on all variables were collected and presented in Table 2.16.

At first blush Table 2.16 appears to be somewhat overwhelming, and any concrete reactions a far cry from the hopeful expectations stated above. On the other hand a close inspection of the table reveals that on variables like costs and labour turnover the range in each case was large. Wide variations such as these are certainly noteworthy but because of the problem of comparing fundamentally different kinds of measures it was convenient to convert the raw data in Table 2.16 to ranked data. This has been done in Table 2.17

Table 2.16

Assessment of all sections on the organisational variables

Sections	Organisational variables									
	P	Q	C	JSE	JSS	WA	Ac	Ab	LT	LU
a	3	− 6.4	−41.0	14	7	6.0	0.00	1	16.7	0
b	8	−10.7	25.6	21	9	5.9	0.03	9	27.6	0
c	28	− 2.2	10.5	4	14	5.3	0.00	8	31.8	0
d	15	4.3	3.9	12	11	7.0	0.00	7	8.0	0
e	21	17.5	7.2	18	13	5.2	0.11	2	15.8	0
f	10	9.0	50.8	24	6	7.8	0.00	6	38.1	1
g	3	− 2.3	− 6.5	10	3	4.7	0.00	5	4.4	0
h	18	8.2	5.0	8	8	4.7	0.00	13	19.0	0
i	6	11.0	44.2	26	10	5.6	0.04	14	52.7	5
j	12	− 7.7	−27.4	6	4	2.4	0.00	4	21.7	0
k	26	−25.5	4.2	21	1	6.9	0.07	10	27.6	0
1	24	2.9	− 2.5	28	12	7.5	0.00	12	45.0	0
m	21	−10.1	− 5.0	16	5	5.4	0.00	11	36.6	0
n	15	− 2.6	36.6	2	2	2.7	0.00	3	0.0	0

P = production: a ranking of the sections's ability to achieve targets. (Rankings doubled because of tied ranks.)

Q = quality: achievement with respect to budget.

C = costs: achievement with respect to budget.

JSE = job satisfaction of employees: overall ranking of sections on 10 different job aspects. (Rankings doubled because of tied ranks.)

JSS = job satisfaction of supervisors: overall ranking of sections on 10 different job aspects.

WA = work anxiety: incidence of work anxiety on a 16 point scale.

Ac = accidents: average frequency per employee of reportable lost-time accidents.

Ab = absence: overall rankings of sections on 4 different measures of absenteeism.

LT = labour turnover: rate of labour turnover the six month period.

IU = industrial unrest: numbers of failures-to-agree over the six month period.

Note: This table used ranked data when these were the only primary data available. Low scores indicate favourable conditions.

where an overall ranking of the sections has been obtained from the sum of ranks.

The advantage of Table 2.17 is that it presents the data in such a way that a general pattern in the results is immediately recognisable, with sections on the left hand side of the table tending to have low ranks, and sections on the right hand side of the table typically having high ranks. This meant that sections not only differed from each other but tended to do so consistenly with respect to these variables.

Connection between variables

Table 2.17 enabled the interrelationships between the variables to be examined more closely, and the following results were obtained.

Within sections there was a tendency for rankings on production, quality and costs to be positively correlated, although this relationship was not significant statistically ($W = 0.44$, $X^2 = 16.99$ with 13 df, $p < 0.20$).

Rankings on job satisfaction of employees, job satisfaction of supervisors and work anxiety were also correlated, and this relationship was statistically significant ($W = 0.60$, $X^2 = 23.50$ with 13 df, $p < 0.05$).

Rankings on accidents, absence, labour turnover and industrial unrest, while tending to correlate, were not statistically significant ($W = 0.38$, $X^2 = 19.52$ with 13 df, $p < 0.20$).

Cross-sectional consistency

When all the variables appearing in Table 2.17 were considered together the effects previously noted appeared to be additive, and there was a strong inclination for all rankings within sections to be similar ($W = 0.30$, $X^2 = 38.83$ with 13 df, $p < 0.001$).

There were four low-ranking sections in which the interconnection between the variables was most evident, namely, 'g', 'j', 'n' and 'a'; and three high-ranking sections, 'f', 'l' and 'i' in which it was also prominent. In the intermediate group of sections ranking also tended to be similar but towards the middle of the scales.

Sections with generally low ranks tended to be reliable in meeting production requirements, to have low costs of manufacture, and to have relatively good standards of workmanship. The members of the sections, including both supervisors and employees, tended to have high levels of job satisfaction and low levels of work anxiety. These

Table 2.17

Ranking of all sections on each variable

Variable	Section													
	g	j	n	a	m	d	h	b	k	c	e	f	l	i
Production	1.5	6	7.5	1.5	10.5	7.5	9	4	13	14	10.5	5	12	3
Quality	7	4	6	5	3	10	11	2	1	8	14	12	9	13
Costs	3	2	12	1	4	6	8	11	7	10	9	14	5	13
Job satisfaction of employees	5	3	1	7	8	6	4	10.5	10.5	2	9	12	14	13
Job satisfaction of supervisors	3	4	2	7	5	11	8	9	1	14	13	6	12	10
Work anxiety	3.5	1	2	10	7	12	3.5	9	11	6	5	14	13	8
Accidents	5.5	5.5	5.5	5.5	5.5	5.5	5.5	11	13	5.5	14	5.5	5.5	12
Absence	5	4	3	1	11	7	13	9	10	8	2	6	12	14
Labour trunover	2	7	1	5	11	3	6	8.5	8.5	4	4	12	13	14
Industrial unrest	6.5	6.5	6.5	6.5	6.5	6.5	6.5	6.5	6.5	6.5	6.5	13	6.5	14
Sum of ranks	42	43	46.5	49.5	71.5	74.5	74.5	80.5	81.5	84	87	99.5	102	114

Note: In this table high rankings indicate adverse effects, for example, high costs of manufacture, high levels of job dissatisfaction, high labour turnover.

units were comparatively stable as indicated by the rates of absence and labour turnover.

For sections with high ranks the picture was significantly different. Performance with respect to quality and costs was generally low . There was a considerable amount of dissatisfaction within these sections, and many employees experienced relatively high levels of work anxiety. With a tendency for there to be relatively high rates of absence and labour turnover, or high incidence of industrial unrest, the sections could be considered to be organisationally unstable.

Conclusions

(1) Wide and consistent differences were found between the organisational units or sections of this company.

(2) Separate measures of performance, satisfaction and stability, respectively, tended to be related, although it was only in the case of satisfaction that the relationship was found to be significant.

(3) When all measures were taken together these tendencies were cumulative, so that within units the variables were interelated, indicating that the latter were linked by an underlying structure. This was reflected in the property of cross-sectional consistency.

(4) The results also indicated that the sections could be separated into two distinct groups. In one group sections were generally capable of attaining satisfactory standards in all performance areas: production, quality and costs. The members of these sections, including both supervisors and employees, tended to have high levels of job satisfaction and low levels of work anxiety. These units were organisationally stable as indicated by their rates of absence and labour turnover.

(5) In the second group the sections exhibited a profile which was significantly different. Within these units considerable dissatisfaction and high levels of work anxiety prevailed. Organisationally the units were unstable, with high rates of absence and labour turnover, or a high incidence of industrial unrest. Achievement on at least one of the performance measures was seriously inadequate.

Notes

1. This experience provided a clinical background against which the data were interpreted.

2. One limitation to this approach of assessing cost effectiveness was that 'hidden' cost, due to accidents or labour turnover for example, could not be accounted for. Measures incorporating these elements would be much more expensive to derive.

3. It will be observed in Table 2.11 that this measure did not discriminate between the sections. In further research an alternative measure encompassing less serious accidents may reflect differences in accident levels between organisational sub-units.

4. E.g. age, family responsibility, see Liddell (1954), Kahne, Ryder, Snegriff and Wyshak (1957), Shephard and Walker (1958), and Behrend (1959).

5. E.g. Behrend (1953).

6. E.g. too much waiting time, Van Beck (1964); poor promotion opportunities, Patchen (1960); insecurity, Owens (1966).

7. See Woytinsky (1942), Cook (1951).

8. E.g. age, Long (1951); sex, Brissenden and Frankel (1922), Klein (1961); intelligence and aptitude, Viteles (1924), Brown and Ghiselli (1953); interest, Strong (1943), Boyd (1961); personality factors, Fisher and Hanna (1931), Hakkinen and Toivainen (1960); previous length of service, Wickert (1951).

9. E.g. skill, Fisher (1917), Long (1951); job satisfaction, Mosel and Wade (1951), Hulin (1966).

10. E.g. team work, Mayo and Lombard (1944); supervision, Fox and Scott (1953), Fleishman and Harris (1962); management, Raphael et al. (1938); industrial relations, Knowles (1965).

11. These data were also incapble of discriminating between the sections. As discussed later (Chapter 4) alternative measures of unrest tapping the process at earlier stages of development may bring out essential differences between the sections.

3 Dimensions of internal structure

In this chapter the analysis of the results is pursued with a view to examining more closely the basic interrelationships between the data. The aim is to isolate the dimensions out of which the internal structure of the sections is composed and, either by inspection or recourse to the literature, to identify what the constructs might be.

Analysis of internal structure

While the property of concordance was perhaps the most striking feature of Table 2.17 there was a propensity for wide deviations from the general pattern to occur in individual cases. In order to examine and explain this disposition more fully a subsequent analysis was conducted on the raw data where, by employing a more powerful method of analysis, it was hoped that the technique would be robust enough to account for some of these puzzling discrepancies indicated by the ranked data.

Method

By inspection of Table 2.17 it can observed that the variance on accidents and industrial unrest was low, so these variables were discarded from the following analysis. From the remaining data a correlation matrix was developed as shown in Table 3.1.

As these measures were clearly interrelated, factor analysis was employed to order and simplify the correlation with a vew to identifying recognisable combinations of variables. Principal components analysis was the specific technique adopted to condense the matrix of correlations.[1]

Four factors were extracted, all satisfying the criterion that the sums of squares of the factor loadings at least equal unity (Kaiser 1960, Child 1970). The factors are shown in Table 3.2 together with loadings of the variables on these factors.

As expected from the concordance relationship with the ranked data there was a principal component which accounted for a large proportion of total variance (approximatley 39 per cent). By inspection of Table 3.2 again the three remaining components accounted for approximately 19, 15 and 12 per cent of the variance respectively.

Discussion

The preceding analysis revealed that the internal structure of the sections consisted of a social and psychological or behavioural dimension devolving around the principal component, and a performance structure embracing the three remaining factors. On account of the high loadings on these latter factors they could be identified as relating primarily to quality, production and costs respectively. An important feature of these results was that they demonstrated that

Table 3.1

Correlation matrix of organisational variables

Variables	1	2	3	4	5	6	7	8
1. Production								
2. Quality	−13							
3. Costs	00	35						
4. Job satisfaction of employees	−05	12	28					
5. Job satisfaction of supervisors	26	60	08	21				
6. Work anxiety	14	06	18	75	34			
7. Absence	30	−02	31	43	18	33		
8. Labour turnover	19	07	29	71	33	47	67	

Note: Decimal points omitted.

Table 3.2

Principal components analysis of the organisational variables

| Variables | Common factor loadings | | | | Communality |
	I	II	III	IV	h^2
1. Production	14	19	78*	13	68
2. Quality	18	−74*	−02	06	58
3. Costs	25	−21	−26	70*	66
4. Job satisfaction of employees	46*	13	−35*	−26	42
5. Job satisfaction of supervisors	29	−49*	40*	−28	56
6. Work anxiety	44*	11	−12	−44*	41
7. Absence	40*	27	17	38*	41
8. Labour turnover	48*	18	−01	05	27
Latent roots	3.10	1.49	1.19	0.97	
Percentage variance	38.77	18.60	14.88	12.13	

Note: Decimal points omitted.

* denotes significant loadings (values greater than = 0.30).

while the behavioural structure dimension tended to be unified and integrated the performance dimension was more complex and diversified. This meant that if overall effectiveness were to be optimised not only should the performance and the behavioural factors be kept in balance, but also a balance needed to be struck between competing performance objectives.

These results were slightly at variance with earlier conclusions reached by Woodward (1965). In the latter study it was reported from interview that some line supervisors found it impossible to meet schedules and still maintain the required quality standards, or keep within the standard costs, suggesting that production was inversely related to either or both quality and costs. In the present research the empirical relationships were found to be more complex than this, since the sections with good production records were different from those maintaining higher quality standards, and different again from those with sound cost performances.

Although the three performance factors were independent in the manner just described, each had important implications regarding job satisfaction. For example, where quality was high, supervisory job satisfaction was also high, indicating how achievement was conducive to the development of positive attitudes. Similarly supervisory job satisfaction and production were also positively linked, again showing how pairs of variables could be mutually supporting.

With the employees, however, these kinds of relationships did not exist. Instead, the level of employee job satisfaction seemed to be independent of quality achievement, and in fact inversely related to production achievement. That is, in this company production targets appeared to be achieved at the expense of employee job satisfaction.

The same kind of inverse relationship existed between costs and both employee and supervisory job satisfaction, where again there was a tendency for the former to be achieved at the expense of the latter, only in this case the relationship was weaker and did not meet normal requirements for statistical significance. On the other hand, as Table 3.2 shows, absence was significantly related to costs, and low absenteeism was conducive to economical costs of production.

The central role of achievement in affecting the job satisfaction of supervisors is a point which will be taken up in Chapter 4, but by way of recapitulation at this stage emphasis should be placed upon the complex nature of organisational performance. The practical implications are important, for the results suggest that the managerial neccessity is to balance and reconcile demands competing in three independent directions. When goals relating to social/psychological issues are added to these performance requirements the managerial task becomes challenging almost beyond reasonableness.

Behavioural structure

From the principal components analysis it was possible to determine the scores for each section on the social/psychological factor, and these are shown in Table 3.3.

Table 3.3

Scores for each section on principal component

n	j	g	a	h	d	e	c	k	m	b	f	i	l
2.81	2.54	2.05	1.61	0.04	0.02	−0.07	−0.31	−0.34	−0.39	−0.68	−1.81	−2.71	−2.77

Whereas the performance structure of the sections could be differentiated into components which could be recognised specifically as relating to production, quality and costs paradoxically this social/psychological dimension could not be so readily labelled, in spite of its more simplified and unified composition. To assist in its identification recourse was made to the literature where several major dimensions of work and organisational behaviour have been established.

Personnel function of management

The importance of the personnel function of management, for example, has long been recognised (Twenty Personnel Executives 1947). Perhaps the most detailed analysis of this function has been provided by Pigors and Myers (1956), although its significance is being constantly re-examined and has emerged most recently as management's human resources function (Bakke 1960). Notwithstanding the metamorphosis, the concept still serves to encompass line management's responsibility for its human resources and the role established by the personnel or industrial relations department:

Mackenzie (1966) neatly distinguished between the personnel function of management and the function of personnel management to illustrate the differentiation. Since the assumptions that managers make about the nature of people determine their managerial strategies (Schein 1965), within the personnel function of managment a clear distinction can be made between Theory X and Theory Y type strategies (McGregor 1960). Also, within the function of personnel management four distinct kinds of roles may be established by personnel departments: a counterbalancing role aimed at meeting deficiencies of line managers on personnel matters; a bureaucratic orientation where emphasis is placed on procedure and detail, where means are valued at the expense of ends; a consultative role in which line and staff work together to solve problems of mutual interest; and a catalytic role leading to organisational development or other forms of planned change (Myers 1970, Levinson 1970). Because of the mutual interactions between the two sets of activities the full utilisation of the personnel function depends upon development in both directions as well as upon their successful integration.

The human organisation

In an alternative way Likert (1967) used the concept of the human organisation to embrace the sum total of the organisation's human assets, of which the causal and intervening variables form specific sub-sets (Likert 1961, Seashore 1964). Likert identified four types of management systems, differing according to the source of pressure applied to achieve productivity goals, the presence or absence of supportive relationships, the nature of communication, whether interpersonal relationships embodied trust and confidence or fear, and whether or not output and quality goals were internalised. These different kinds of strategies have different consequences, as evidenced by the end result variables, shown previously in Figure 2.2.

Organisational climate

In contrast with these managerial orientations a different perspective is provided by the term organisational climate. This refers to the set of characteristic which are relatively enduring over time, typifying an organisation and distinguishing it from other organisations. This collection of characteristics creates a distinctive atmosphere or psychological climate within the organisation (Pritchard and Karasick 1973), which influences the behaviour of its members (Forehand and Gilmer 1964). In a perceptive critique of the concept Guion (1973) saw it as a pervasive set of variables impinging upon the person at work. Because of the difficulty in defining and isolating the constituent varaibles he profored to regard it as a construct, or family of constructs, and held the concept to be one of the most exciting developments in organisational psychology in recent years.

Steady state

Another affinity exists between the concept of organisational climate and the identification of steady state in social instiutions, attributable to the early work of the Tavistock Institute of Human Relations. One of the aims of this research was to examine the psychological and social forces affecting the group life, morale and produc tivity of a single industrial community or factory (Jaques 1950). As the research developed it focused upon labour turnover as a distinctive social process by means of which the organisation both replaced its leavers and accommodated to the consequent continuous change in the composition of its labour force. Frequency (survival) distributions were used as indicators of these activities, and the regularity of the distribution revealed the quasi-stationary nature of the process (Rice, Hill and Trist 1950). Internal crisis, such as threat of redundancy, was preceded by a tendency for employees to stay on longer in the firm than they did formerly, but the survival pattern returned to its previous level after the period of disturbance was over (Hill 1951). This indicated that the survival process and the underlying social processess operated during this time as self-regulating mechanisms.

Within the factory they studed departments, divisions or otherwise named sections were identified in field theory terms as bounded regions. Again the labour turnover process was found to provide an indication of the degree of differentiation of these boundaries with those sub-units which had lower labour turnover rates also possessing the more highly structured boundaries (Rice 1951, Rice and Trist 1952).

Irrespective of the constancy of the organisational processes, when these were fundamentally modified by altering the factory organisation and policy so that the whole cultural, political and power structure in the organisation was changed (Jaques 1951), there was a concomitant change in the labour turnover process and the rate of labour turnover of the organisation (Rice and Trist 1952).

Synthesis

It is apparent that many overlapping aspects exist between these four concepts and the social/psychological factor identified in the present analysis. While it was beyond the scope of this research to reach out and incorporate these other dimensions of organisational functioning it is suggested that concepts such as the personnel function of management and the human organisation emphasise process considerations while organisational climate, as defined by Payne, Fineman and Wall (1976), and steady state, focus attention on structural properties. In any event the managerial and organisational forces will have behavioural repercussions and it is tentatively proposed that the social/psychological factor identified in the present analysis is a useful way of representing the constructs resulting from these complex interactions. This possibility will be examined in Chapter 4.

Conclusions

(1) The internal structure of the organisational units was found to be composed of a relatively simplified and unified behavioural factor or construct, and a more complex performance structure relating to production, quality and costs.

(2) From a managerial perspective the results suggested that besides achieving a balance between performance and behavioural factors, balance also needs to be struck between competing performance objectives.

(3) For purposes of identificaton the highly integrated behavioural factor was compared with other dimensions of organisational functioning reported in the literature, of which the personnel function of management, the human organisation, organisational climate, and steady state were identified as being of predominant significance. While it was apparent that many affinities existed between the behavioural factor and these other constructs further research would be required to reveal more precisely the degree to which they were interrelated.

Notes

1   The BMD (OIM) programme of the University of California was used to make this analysis.

4   Composition of behavioural structure

The identification of a behavioural construct as a constituent dimension of organisational functioning had important implications for the variables chosen for this study.   These implications were explored by examining the strength of the relationship between the behavioural factor and each of the organisational variables.   The most significant of these relationships involved labour turnover, job satisfaction of employees and work anxiety, and to a lesser degree absence and job satisfaction of supervisors.   Since the raw data on accidents and industrial unrest were incomplete the relevance of the behavioural factor for these variables could not be empirically established, so an attempt was made to indicate the significance of these relationships by interpreting other results reported in the literature within the context of the findings of the present research.

Relevance of the behavioural construct

In the previous analysis a behavioural factor was identified which interrelated the social and psychological characteristics typifying but distinguishing the sections, and it remained to examine the implications that this construct may have had for each of the organisational variables. The method adopted to clarify these relationships was to relate each variable in turn to all the other variables taken together, using principal components analysis again to identify the primary dimension linking the constellation of variables in each case. This slightly elaborate procedure ensured that any variable was not being correlated with a construct within which it was already embedded.

To take production as an example, a principal components analysis was conducted on the remaining set of variables to obtain factor scores for all sections on this component, and these scores were correlated with the scores pertaining to each section on the production measure. The correlation so obtained indicated the extent to which differences between the sections with respect to this measure were accounted for primarily by the consistent differences between the sections relating to their behavioural structure.

This method was repeated isolating each variable in turn; Table 4.1 summarises the results. In each case the principal component was interpreted as corresponding to the behavioural construct identified in Chapter 3.

Table 4.1 shows that the relationship between the behavioural construct and each of the performance variables was statistically not significant, so further consideration of performance was deferred until Chapter 5. In contrast the behavioural construct accounted for a large part of the differences between the sections in labour turnover, job satisfaction of employees and work anxiety. In addition a hint of promise could be attached to both absence and job satisfaction of supervisors, for although the relationships were not statistically significant the connections were strong enough to raise the question as to whether or not higher levels of association could be identified if the properties of these variables were to be taken into account. With this end in mind further analyses of all the social/psychological variables were undertaken. At the same time an overview of previous research on each variable was conducted. This was necessitated by the nature of the variables with which we were dealing: if they themselves were complex it would be important to turn

Table 4.1

Table of correlations between each variable and the factor scores of the sections on the principal component relating to the remaining set of variables

Variable	Remaining set of variables			
	r	t	df	p<
P	0.17	0.60	12	NS
Q	0.20	0.70	12	NS
C	0.33	1.24	12	NS
JSE	0.66	3.02	12	0.05
JSS	0.36	1.33	12	NS
WA	0.58	2.49	12	0.05
Ab	0.47	1.82	12	NS
LT	0.71	3.50	12	0.01

to the literature in order to determine the many kinds of factors shaping or influencing them.

Job satisfaction of employees

While the primary intention of administering the job satisfaction questionnaire was to obtain a measure of satisfaction for each of the 14 sections this led, as Table 2.6 shows, to the collection of much information in the area of job satisfaction itself, and these data could now be analysed in the hope that further insights into the nature of job satisfaction could be developed. The concordance relationship reported in Table 2.7 was of particular interest, so it was appropriate to return to the raw data appearing in Table 2.6 and from this to form the correlation matrix shown in Table 4.2.

Table 4.2 confirmed that a number of interrelationships existed between the scale scores so again principal components analysis was employed to condense the matrix of correlations to see if the scores were connected in any essential way. Using the normal criterion two factors were extracted, as shown in Table 4.3. The loadings of the variables on these factors are also shown.

All variables had loadings on the first factor which accounted for 48 per cent of total variance. The second factor accounted for 22 per cent of variance. Factor scores for all sections were obtained on these two factors, as shown in Table 4.4.

Factor identification

From Table 4.4 it can be observed that sections 'n', 'c' and 'j' had high scores on the principal component, with low scores registered by sections 'f', 'l' and 'I'. These findings confirmed the results obtained previously with the ranked data (Table 2.7). So as to assist in the identification of this factor the sections' scores shown in Table 4.4 were correlated with the scores relating to the behavioural construct previously isolated: the correspondence between the two sets of measures was high ($r = 0.74$, $p < 0.01$, see Table 4.10).

Although the first factor turned out to be of primary interest to the central theme of the research it should be noted that the second factor exhibited in Table 4.4 also subsumed a sizable percentage of the variance. This factor indicated that some sections (especially 'a', 'h', 'I' and 'd') had favourable attitudes towards supervision and

Table 4.2

Correlation matrix of job satisfaction aspects for employees

Job Aspect	1	2	3	4	5	6	7	8	9	10
1. Com										
2. C & M	14									
3. PWC	54	52								
4. Se	42	62	70							
5. So	74	−07	10	22						
6. Su	68	−18	27	21	61					
7. W	78	29	80	70	41	53				
8. WE	06	43	31	06	−15	−41	13			
9. WI	47	49	40	78	53	24	50	13		
10. WV	64	14	60	52	56	33	67	01	48	

Note: Decimal points omitted.

Table 4.3

Principal components analysis of the job aspects for employees

Job aspects	Common factor loadings		Communality
	I	II	h²
1. Com	38*	−22	19
2. C & M	20	48*	23
3. PWC	36*	22	18
4. Se	36*	28	21
5. So	28	−38*	22
6. Su	25	−45*	27
7. W	41*	02	17
8. WE	05	48*	23
9. WI	34*	10	12
10. WV	36*	−10	13
Latent rots	4.81	2.19	
Percentage variance	4812	21.89	

Note: Decimal points omitted.

    * = significant loadings.

Table 4.4

Scores for each section on first two factors
(job satisfaction of employees)

Section	Scores on first two factors	
	I	II
a	0.93	−4.39
b	−0.84	0.39
c	2.63	0.87
d	0.36	−0.10
e	−0.60	1.60
f	−.171	−0.03
g	0.94	0.04
h	1.91	−1.30
i	−2.22	0.23
j	2.37	1.84
k	−1.30	0.14
l	−4.96	−0.19
m	− 0.51	0.51
n	3.00	0.39

fellow employees, in contrast to other sections (namely 'm', 'c', 'e' and 'j') which had favourable attitudes towards company and management. While this suggested that employees in some sections derived support from their colleagues or their supervisors, and in other sections they turned towards management and the company as a source of satisfaction, further research would be necessary to take up this point more fully.

Interconnection of attitudes

The most striking feature of Table 2.7 was the consistency in attitudes between sections, i.e. the tendency in one group of sections for most employees to see the job aspects as being comparatively satisfactory, while in another group these job aspects were generally regarded as being unsatisfactory.

This effect was illustrated in three ways. Firstly, these differences occurred with respect to job aspects such as physical working conditions, security, and work variety, all of which could be considered to be generally uniform throughout the whole division. That is, in spite of the fact that these job aspects were comparable in all sections, satisfaction with regard to them varied widely, and related to the overall level of satisfaction in each section. Secondly, on some job aspects a difference of opinion would normally be expected, such as with supervision, for each section was controlled by a different supervisor. But again in this case it will be noted that the satisfaction felt towards the supervisors corresponded closely with the overall level of job satisfaction prevailing in the sections. Lastly, on wages, it was possible to compare the levels of satisfaction with the actual wages received. The results showed that the levels of satisfaction with wages did not correlate with the actual wage levels ($r = -0.12$). Instead, differences in satisfaction with wages again were consistent with the overall pattern of difference in satisfaction between sections.

It can now be seen that the concordance relationship depicted by the data, embracing wide and consistent differences between sections, pointed towards an interconnection of attitudes within sections. This result was confirmed by factor analysis with the principal component accounting for a major proportion of the variance.

Previous research into job satisfaction

Historically, from the early studies of Kornhauser (1930) and Hoppock (1935) to the research undertaken by Herzberg, Mausner,

Peterson and Capwell (1957) heavy emphasis was placed upon the job as a source of satisfaction. With many of these and subsequent studies the aim was to identify specific job aspects related to job satisfaction, and to determine actual levels of satisfaction experienced by employees on the various job aspects (e.g. Schultz 1964, Mountain 1965, Porter and Lawler 1965, O'Brien 1966, Lahiri and Srivastva 1967, Monie 1967, Cameron 1969, Ryder 1969, Warr and Routledge 1969).

Concurrently it was also recognised that certain personal characteristics could intrude upon the relationship between a person and his job, and that satisfaction was dependent upon personality factors, intelligence and aptitude, age and tenure (e.g. Fisher and Hanna 1931, Ghiselli 1953,Walker and Lumsden 1963). More recently the influence of social background has been examined. For example, different attitudes to work have been found to exist between city and small-town factory workers (Hulin 1966, Turner and Lawrence 1967, and Hulin and Blood 1968). In addition Silverman (1970) and Vaughan and Gardner (1976) found that employees brought different expectations to work according to their social class work values and job satisfaction was dependent upon these initial expectations.

Notwithstanding the strong influence that the job has in determining satisfaction, and the way this may be modified by personal characteristics, it was also apparent that satisfaction was influneced by organisational characteristics. Apart from the comprehensive research into leadership which is well documented, organsational structure also emerged as an important factor. For example in their review of the literature Porter and Lawler (1965) found that differences in attitude were related to organisational level, line/staff hierarchy, sub-unit size, total-organisation size, and centralised/decentralised shape.

One of the current issues in the field is the relative importance of job characteristics and structural variables in explaining differences in attitudes. Perhaps the problem may be most clearly outlined by contrasting the research of Herman and Hulin (1973) with that of Stone and Porter (1975). In the former case a sample of some 300 managers from a large manufacturing company was taken and it was found that while differences in attitudes could be accounted for partly in terms of personal characteristics (age, tenure, educational level), the greater influence was exercised by the structural variables: type of department (task specialisation), functional division (production,

production services, staff), and level in the hierarchy. As Herman and Hulin concluded the results demonstrated that attitudes were highly associated with the individual's position within the organisational structure.

Stone and Porter, however, noted that the kinds of jobs represented in this study varied considerably, and that the differences shown in attitudes could have been a reflection of this rather than task specialisation, function, or hierarchical level. Accordingly they took some 600 blue and white collar workers in a telephone company, all holding jobs at the same hierarchical level. When indeed attitudes were found to vary between jobs it was concluded that job duties were more instrumental in determining attitudes than were structural factors involving department, function, or rank.

In the present research it has been seen that the results could not be accounted for either by rank or by job: like the Stone and Porter study all the jobs were at the same hierarchical level, but in contrast to their study wide differences between the jobs did not exist. Moreover, and more significantly, attitudes to physical working conditions had little to do with extant physical working conditions, attitudes to pay bore little relationship to actual levels of pay, and so on. Rather, as has been shown, the prevailing attitudes corresponded with conditions that were more fundamental and pervasive. By way of summary it may be said that the data indicated that in this company the level of job satisfaction experienced with respect to a particular job aspect was associated not so much with characteristics of that job aspect taken in isolation, but more with the nature of the behavioural structure of the sections in which the employees worked.

Conclusions

(1) Wide differences were found in the levels of job satisfaction prevailing between the 14 sections in which all the employees were at the same hierarchical level, and all were employed in work calling for light, repetitive manual skills.

(2) Within sections job satisfaction scores on different job aspects were interrelated, so that one group of sections tended to be characterised by relatively favourable attitudes regarding the job aspects, and another group tended to exhibit generally unfavourable attitudes on the same job aspects.

(3) The interconnection of attitudes pointed towards the existence of endemic conditions within the sections which determined the disparity and consistency in levels of satisfaction.

(4) These consistent differences in the levels of job satisfaction between the sections could be largely accounted for by a single factor embracing the behavioural structure of the sections in which the employees worked.

(5) This finding was in marked contrast to previous research which emphasised the importance of job, formal structure, and societal factors as determinants of satisfaction at work.

Job satisfaction of supervisors

Since the results obtained from the preliminary analysis of the supervisory data tended to follow a pattern similar to that obtained with the employee questionnaire a further analysis was also undertaken on the supervisory results, again repeating the method of analysis just utilised.   Thus a correlation matrix was developed from Table 2.8 and this is shown in Table 4.5.

Again using principal components analysis and the conventional criterion for choosing factors, four were extracted as shown in Table 4.6.

It will be noted from Table 4.6 that the principal component not only accounted for approximately 26 per cent of variance, but recorded significant loadings on seven of the job aspects, confirming its operation as a general factor affecting the attitudes of the supervisors.

With respect to the second factor shown in Table 4.6, the method of analysis was to correlate the factor scores of the sections on this component with the factor scores of the sections on the behavioural structure component.   The correlation was significant ($r = 0.69$, $p < 0.01$, see Table 4.10).

A similar approach was used to identify the third factor shown in Table 4.6, only this time it was costs which provided the positive correlation ($r = 0.48$, $p < 0.05$). This technique, however, was not successful in labelling the fourth factor shown in Table 4.6, and its identity remained unknown.

Nature of supervisory attitudes

Because of the results obtained on a number of the other variables it was not surprising to find that wide differences in the levels of job satisfaction existed between the supervisors (Table 2.8).   This effect was most clearly seen in Table 2.9 which highlighted the consistency

Table 4.5

Correlation matrix of job satisfaction aspects for supervisors

Job aspect	1	2	3	4	5	6	7	8	9	10
1. Com										
2. Coy	41									
3. PWC	−06	32								
4. Se	43	39	00							
5. So	23	28	−03	44						
6. Mgt	05	11	53	06	28					
7. W	−15	20	64	09	−32	45				
8. WE	−41	09	22	−16	01	−35	−04			
9. WI	28	−08	26	−08	08	57	−00	−02		
10. WV	−07	06	02	−32	−34	−23	15	04	−33	

Note: Decimal points omitted.

Table 4.6

Principal components analysis of the job aspects for supervisors

| Job aspect | Common factor loadings | | | | Communality |
	I	II	III	IV	h²
1. Com	32*	34*	13	37*	37
2. Coy	32*	05	56*	−09	43
3. PWC	33*	−49*	15	−18	40
4. Se	34*	32*	31*	−04	32
5. So	31*	25	−00	−38*	36
6. Mgt	47*	−27	−29	09	39
7. W	22	−52*	24	17	41
8. WE	−17	−17	17	−73*	62
9. WI	32*	−10	−51*	−05	38
10. WV	−26	−22	36*	34	36
Latent roots	2.56	2.13	1.56	1.29	
Percentage variance	25.58	21.35	15.59	12.94	

Note: Decimal points omitted.

   * = significant loadings.

in attitudes between supervisors, i.e. the tendency for some super-visors to regard most of the job aspects satisfactorily, while others generally saw these same job aspects as being unsatisfactory. This result mirrored that obtained with employee job satisfaction: since job aspects such as company, security and work variety, for example, could be considered to be uniform for the whole division, wide dif-ferences in attitudes to these aspects would not usually be expected; yet the fact that satisfaction with regard to these job aspects did vary widely pointed to the existence of underlying conditions determining these attitudes, especially since the satisfaction actually experienced on the specific aspects related to the overall levels of satisfaction affecting the supervisors.

On the other hand with a job aspect such as management, dif-ferences in attitudes could normally be expected, since each super-visor would have developed a different relationship with the divi-sional manager, and to the particular managers to which they indivi-dually reported. In this case, however, it will be observed that the satisfaction that each supervisor felt towards management again corresponded closely with the general level of satisfaction experi-enced by that supervisor. This concordance relationship demon-strated an interconnection of attitudes characterising the supervisors in this company, and this result was confirmed by multivariate analy-sis with the principal component showing significant loadings on seven of the job aspects.

Relevance of behavioural structure

Table 4.6 also showed that differences in the level of satisfaction between the sections could in part be accounted for by differences in the behavioural structure characterising the sections. Thus super-visory job satisfaction tended to be high in those sections which were stable (low accidents, absence, labour turnover and industrial unrest) and displayed high levels of employee job satisfaction. This indi-cated that behavioural structure could play an important role in influencing satisfaction at work although further research would be necessary to investigate more thoroughly the nature of this relation-ship, especially the direction of causality.

Significance of performance

As previously noted, Table 4.6 showed that differences in satisfac-tion between the supervisors could be accounted for in part by differences in the cost performance of the sections for which the supervisors were responsible. Furthermore, as previously noted in connection with Table 3.2, a strong connection also existed between satisfaction and achievement relating to production and quality. Where the quality of the work was good, or the work was performed reliably so that production targets were consistently achieved, the supervisors in charge of such sections tended to sustain high levels of satisfaction.

Thus with respect to all three performance criteria the results showed that achievement and satisfaction were closely interrelated. It was beyond the scope of the present research to say whether the favourable attitudes were conducive to high performance, or whether achievement led to higher satisfaction, and further research would be necessary to probe the directional effects of the relationship. The results were, however, consistent with the idea that performance and satisfaction were mutually reinforcing.

Conclusions

(1) Wide differences were found in the levels of satisfaction between the 14 supervisors in this company who all performed similar duties.

(2) For each supervisr job satisfaction scores on different job aspects were interrelated, so that while some supervisors tended to have favourable attitudes towards most of the job aspects, others tended to have negative attitudes regarding these same job aspects.

(3) The interconnection of attitudes indicated that satisfaction arose not so much from the job aspects taken in isolation, but more from other factors located in the working and organisational environment.

(4) The results suggested that satisfaction was closely related to performance — in this case to achievement regarding production, quality or costs — so that dissatisfaction arose when performance in the section controlled by a supervisor was inadequate on any of these criteria.

(5) The results also indicated that satisfaction was closely related to behavioural structure, so that satisfaction tended to be high in sections characterised by a structure embracing stability and favourable attitudes.

Work anxiety

As Table 2.10 shows the level of anxiety in the sections ranged from a scale score of 2.4 in section 'j' to 7.8 in section 'f'. In order to establish the significance of this range of scores it was convenient to refer to Table 3.1 which indicates that the correlation between work anxiety and job dissatisfaction was high ($r = 0.75$, $p < 0.01$), showing that in sections characterised by favourable attitudes low levels of anxiety prevailed, and that high levels of anxiety tended to be sustained in sections pervaded by widespread dissatisfaction.

The significance of the work anxiety data was perhaps best illustrated by the procession of deterioration in organisational functioning, where it was evident that the more dysfunctional the organisational unit the higher was the incidence of anxiety ($r = 0.58$, $p < 0.05$, Table 2.1). Presumably the creation of anxiety formed one stage in the process which resulted in the greater withdrawal behaviour characterising these more stressful work situations.

As mentioned previously, the ways by which work functions as a source of satisfaction have been well researched, but its capacity to act as a source of pressure and conflict which affects health has been far less extensively examined. Early research in this area dealt with the incidence of mental health impairment rather than its causes. For example in a survey conducted by Fraser (1947) a sample of approximately 3,000 male and female factory employees were given a battery of psychological tests, an interview with a social worker, and a medical and psychological examination. It was found that 20 per cent of the employees showed evidence of minor neurosis and 10 per cent suffered from severe neurosis. Neurotic illness was considered to account for between a quarter and a third of all absence from work due to illness.

In a recent survey of the literature relating to coronary heart disease and mental ill health Cooper and Marshall (1976) quote two studies complementing this evidence. In research by Felton and Cole (1963) it was estimated that all cardiovascular diseases accounted for some 12 per cent of the time lost by the US labour force. Also, Aldridge (1970) calculated that the sum of incapacity for men suffering from mental, psychoneurotic and personality disorders, nervousness, debility, and migraine headache, accounted for 22.8 million work days lost in the UK in a single year (1968). From these studies it is evident that the impairment of health is extensive and represents a considerable national cost both in human and financial terms.

Stress is emerging as one of the major causative factors, where it has been called an 'unlisted' occupational hazard (Margolis, Kroes and Quinn 1974). What is important as far as prevention is concerned is to identify the sources of stress, especially with a view to establishing those factors which come under managerial or other control.

Some factors have their origins outside the organisation, such as domestic or family problems (Pahl and Pahl 1971, Tredgold 1972) or crisis (Dohrenwend and Dohrenwend 1974). Others relate to personality, involving individual differences in the ability to cope with pressures and conflicts (Finn, Hickey and O'Doherty 1969, Jenkins 1971). Different kinds of jobs produce different kinds of demands, which in turn produce particular patterns of physiological and psychological responses, e.g. air traffic controllers (Marcson 1970, Shephard 1971, Cobb and Rose 1973). Lastly there are factors of an organisational nature: whether or not people feel that they work under pressure has been linked with leadership style (Busk 1972), and poor mental health has been related to close supervision and little opportunity to exercise autonomy (Quinn, Seashore and Mangione 1971).

While it has been common to find that stress experiences at work have been related to personality factors, to the nature of the job, and even to pressures arising from the domestic situation, in contrast the significance of organisational factors has not been fully established. It was this latter category of factors which concerned the present research, where the aim was to examine the connection between internal structure and work neurosis, in this case called work anxiety.

As the results showed, varying levels of work anxiety were found in the sections analysed in this company. Furthermore, differences between the sections in the level of work anxiety were consistently related to differences between the sections in their internal structures: work anxiety tended to be high in those sections characterised by a behavioural structure associated with dissatisfaction (of both employees and supervisors) and instability (high absenteeism and labour turnover).

Conclusions

(1) Differences in the levels of work anxiety between the 14 sections from this company were found to be related to the type of behavioural structure characterising these sections.

(2) In those sections in which the behavioural structure had

deteriorated employees were prone to higher levels of work anxiety than in sections characterised by a more cohesive and supportive behavioural structure.

(3) These results indicated that further research is need to examine the extent to which (sub.) organisations act as sources of stress leading to the impairment of occupational health.

Absence

On account of the concordance relationship found between the separate measures of absenteeism it was again convenient to use principal components analysis to examine more thoroughly the inter-relationships between these measures. As an intermediate step a correlation matrix was derived from Table 2.13, as shown in Table 4.7.

Table 4.7

Correlation matrix for different absence measures

Type of absence	1	2	3	4
Certificated absence				
1. Hours				
2. Frequency	62			
Uncertificated absence				
3. Hours	05	30		
4. Frequency	07	31	70	

Note: Decimal points omitted.

Using the normal criterion, two factors were extracted from the principal components analysis, as shown in Table 4.8. Factor scores for all sections were obtained on these two factors, and are shown in Table 4.9.

77

Table 4.8

Principle components analysis for the different absence measures

Measure of absenteeism	Common factor loadings		Communality
	I	II	h²
Certificated absence			
1. Hours	40	65	58
2. Frequency	53	42	46
Uncertificated absence			
3. Hours	53	45	48
4. Frequency	54	43	48
Latent roots	2.01	1.31	
Percentage variance	51.21	32.82	

Note: Decimal points omitted.

Table 4.9

Scores for each section on first two factors
(absence analysis)

Factor score	Section													
	a	b	c	d	e	f	g	h	i	j	k	l	m	n
First factor	2.42	−0.24	−0.23	0.51	1.64	0.85	0.46	−1.33	−2.94	1.16	−0.93	−1.19	−0.59	0.92
Second factor	0.76	−0.66	0.55	0.62	−0.46	0.70	−0.63	1.07	−1.20	−1.59	2.09	−1.53	1.21	−0.84

In order that the principal component could be identified the factor scores of the sections on this factor were compared with the corresponding scores obtained in the analysis of behavioural structure, shown in Table 3.2.

The correlation was high ($r = 0.65$, $p < 0.05$), showing that differences between the sections on this absence factor could be accounted for by differences between the sections relating to their behavioural structure.

As for the second factor extracted in Table 4.9 it will be noted that positive loadings were recorded for certificated absence and negative loadings for uncertificated absence. This indicated that bipolar influences operated within the sections, so that in sections 'k', 'm' and 'h' certificated absence tended to be the more familiar way for absenteeism to occur, while in sections 'l', 'j' and 'i' uncertificated absence tended to be more popular.

Discussion

As has been established many factors may cause people to be absent from work (Gaudet 1957, Porter and Steers 1973). Apart from the self-evident influence of sickness, these factors may be classified into three major groups, namely: personal characteristics (e.g. age and family responsibility, Liddell 1954; Kahne, Ryder, Snegriff and Wyshak 1957; Shepherd and Walker 1958; Behrend 1959), external economic conditions (Behrend 1953), and job conditions (e.g. too much waiting time, Van Beck 1964).

To these three major determinants of absence may be added a fourth group involving organisational factors, although the relevance of this group to date has been slower to establish than with the others. Part of the evidence is anecdotal. For example, Isambert-Jamati (1962) described a case recounted by Veil (1960) involving a clinic which employed a majority of women, and consisted of two parallel departments with the same absence rates.

> It was noted that, when a third department was set up by the management, drawing lots from among employees of the first two departments, absenteeism rose sharply in this third department and reached a very high level, while it remained constant in the other two. Three years later, however, absenteeism had dropped and was at the same level in all three departments.

Differences in the rates of absence affecting organisational sub-units has been reported elsewhere (Kerr, Koppelmeier and Sullivan

1951; Mann and Baumgartel 1952; Waters and Roach 1971; Waters and Roach 1973). Perhaps Crowther's (1957) results most clearly illustrate the general nature of these findings. Here absence rates in a number of divisions of a single company were recorded over a six year period. The results showed that while the absolute rates varied from year to year the trends of absence in all departments tended to follow the same pattern. In the light of Behrend's (1953) research presumedly this meant that when the general level of unemployment rose absence rates in all departments tended to fall, and rise again when unemployment diminished. The stability of the general pattern of absence within the divisions was interpreted as indicating that the rates were influenced by long term characteristics of the divisions.

As mentioned earlier previous research has also tended to suggest that different measures of absence reflected different modes of absenteeism. The present research did not confirm these former findings, but did reveal a fundamental relationship arising from the fact that differences were found in all levels of absenteeism in the sections of this company. It may be the case that where sickness or accidents occurring outside the organisation from the major causes of absence from work the various measures of absenteeism remain unconnected. In the present study, however, the evidence pointed towards a more significant role played by organisationally induced absenteeism, in keeping with the research by Crowther (1957). In contrast to the Crowther research, however, the current study showed that absenteeism was but one facet of a broader problem affecting in a cross-sectional manner a wider set of organisational variables. In this sense absence could be viewed as an endemic, structural and organisationally induced problem.

These findings have important implications concerning the use of absence as a personnel statistic. The results showed that absence reflected the nature of the sections' behavioural structure, so that when this deteriorated, symptomatically it tended to affect all measures of absenteeism. This meant that these measures could in turn be used as valuable personnel statistics for gauging the extent of organisational deterioration, especially if employed in conjunction with other indexes such as labour turnover.

Notwithstanding these structural influences on absenteeism, in one group of sections absence tended to occur through official channels, while in another group it tended to be unsanctioned. Thus these results revealed a propensity for certificated and uncertificated absence to be used as mutually exclusive modes by which employees in this company refrained from attending work. Although this point was not pursued in this study the result is consistent with findings of previous research suggesting that absenteeism is heavily influenced by normative factors (Chadwick-Jones 1978).

Conclusions

(1) Wide differences were recorded in the levels of absence in the 14 sections all engaged in similar light repetitive work.

(2) In one group of sections certificated absence was the more familiar way by which people remained away from work, while in another group uncertificated absence was the more common mode of absenteeism.

(3) Over and above this tendency it was also found that in one group of sections the incidence of all forms of absence tended to be low while in another group higher levels of absence prevailed.

(4) These consistent differences in absence measures between the Sections could be accounted for by a single factor embracing the behavioural structure of the sections in which the employees worked.

(5) This finding was in contrast to previous research which has emphasised the importance of sickness, personal characteristics, changes in economic activity, and certain job conditions in determining the level of absence from work.

Labour turnover

Of all the data shown in Table 2.16 perhaps that relating to labour turnover is the most striking, on account of the wide differences in the rates between the 14 sections, corresponding to a range of from zero to over 100 per cent per annum. Differences such as these help to sharpen the significance of labour turnover as a statistical measure. The usefulness of labour turnover as an index was first established when it was developed to represent the rate of turnover of personnel, whereas previously only the number of vacancies had been available as a personnel statistic. The present research highlighted the relevance of labour turnover as a behavioural measure by illustrating its sensitivity to organisational deterioration.

Traditionally labour turnover has been associated with dissatisfaction, although empirical assessment is probably essential in the first instance if this relationship is to be confirmed with any degree of certainty. For example, in an earlier study by Kerr (1947) it was reported that the plant manager and union officials were in total disagreement as to which departments were highest or lowest in job satisfaction (morale), which would have made it difficult if not impossible to relate dissatisfaction to turnover. In the present study, however, when job satisfaction was objectively measured, the correlation was highly significant statistically ($r = 0.71$, $p < 0.001$).

Research has played an important role in identifying factors making for high turnover and reviews of the literature indicate that it can be linked with well over 50 variables. Broadly speaking these can be classified into four main groups — economic, organisational, job, and personal factors (Knowles 1964, Porter and Steers 1973). Under certain circumstances each of these groups is undoubtedly important. One of the most familiar and recurrent findings in labour turnover research is that the probable length of service of a person in his current job is dependent upon his length of service in his previous jobs. Also, external economic conditions affecting the availability of jobs are of fundamental importance in precipitating people's decisions to leave their current jobs.

On the other hand in the present study external economic conditions affected all sections alike, jobs were similar from one section to another, and the sample was large enough virtually to ensure that personal characteristics of whatever kind were randomly distributed throughout all sections. Yet, in spite of this, inordinately wide differences in turnover existed between the sections pointing, as with the other social/psychological variables, to the relevance of structural influences in determining labour turnover.

Summary

(1) Wide differences were found in the rates of labour turnover between the 14 sections in this company.

(2) Objective measures of dissatisfaction and turnover were highly correlated.

(3) Of all the variables used in this study labour turnover was the most accurate predictor of organisational deterioration, which result enhanced the value of this index as a behavioural measure.

(4) Solutions to labour turnover problems therefore are more likely to be found in substantive programmes of structural

development than in specific personnel practices aimed at remedying particular sources of dissatisfaction.

Accidents

The identification of sections beleaguered by high level of absence and labour turnover was a result which one established could have been expected of accidents too, since a strong connection between accidents and both absence and labout turnover has been identified previously (Hill and Trist 1953). Unfortunately the data in Table 2.16 were unable to discriminate between the sections, although it would have been interesting to observe the pattern of results if a more sensitive measure of accidents had been used.

A brief look at the literature may be helpful in bridging this gap. Traditionally when accident statistics have been gathered the data have normally been presented to denote the various categories of disability or fatality (see Appendix 4). While this type of classification is useful in showing how accidents occur, it is only of limited value in suggesting lines of remedial or preventive action. The key to any such programme must lie with the identification of causative factors, and in this connection considerable research into the nature of occupational accidents has been undertaken.

Much of the early research into the nature of accidents concentrated upon isolating hazards or aspects of the physical working environment which contributed to high accident rates. Extremes of temperature (Vernon 1973), operational congestion (Keenan, Kerr and Sherman 1951), and disease organisms or toxic substances (Kerr 1959) were common aspects. In line with this research attempts were made to reduce these kinds of hazards by establishing safety practices.

A later avenue of research concentrated not upon distinctly physical causes but upon individual differences between people. Impetus in this direction was provided by the finding that some people were more likely to have accidents than others, irrespective of hazards. Slow motor and perceptual speed (Drake 1940), defective vision (Tiffin 1951) and some personality factors constituted this syndrome.

One reason why the importance of personal characteristics tended at first to be overestimated was due to the fact that a small number of people could be expected to have more accidents than others purely by chance (Mintz and Blum 1949). Thus if about 15 per cent of accidents can be attributed to causes of this nature and only about 10 per cent are due to distinctly physical causes (Kerr 1959), it leaves the major part of the variance still to be explained.

In attempting to identify further sources of influence we may turn to a study of Kerr (1950), where it was found that while in a group of 53 departments of a single company accident frequency rates were found to vary from 0.0 to 22.7 per workers per annum, and severity values ranged from 0 to 75 (number of days lost per 1,000 man-hours worked), departments highest in accident frequency were usually above average in accident severity. An allied relationship was found in the Trist research where, besides functioning at a higher output rate, the composite work organisation also maintained a low incidence of accidents, an especially important result in the mining industry.

In summarising these results it can be seen that while inital attempts to curb accidents led employers, trade unions and governments to safeguard machinery and eliminate dangerous substances from production processes, these measures can contain only part of the problem. The greatest gain in accident control from now on may well lie in using accident statistics diagnostically in the first place to identify organisational deterioration, and then developing means of treating the condition rather than the symptom.

Industrial unrest

As with accidents the data on idustrial unrest did not discriminate between the sections, although it was interesting to note that since the instances of failures-to-agree occurred in sections 'f' and 'i', the data on this variable were consistant at one end of the spectrum with the general pattern of the results obtained with the other behavioural variables.

Again the literature may be reviewed to compensate for the paucity of data in this study. In attempting to establish the nature of industrial unrest it is convenient to start with an analysis of issues and strikes. Issues can appear by way of complaint or grievance, and pioneering work in this area was done by Roethlisberger and Dickson(1939). They marshalled an intensive interviewing programme with factory employees in order to examine more closely the nature of work dissatisfaction. In their interviews they found that initially employees were not able to specify precisely the particular source of their dissatisfaction. When, however, they were encouraged to talk freely the employees themselves gained emotional relief from the problem, and additionally in many instances the significance of the complaint was revealed to the critical listener. Roethlisberger and Dickson were thus able to distinguish between what they called the manifest and latent nature of complaint, and in subsequent interviews certain complaints were no longer treated as specific facts but were taken to be indicative or symptomatic of underlying factors needing further attention.

Similar distinctions have been found in the analysis of strike activity. Strikes can involve many issues: wage disputes; hours of work; employment of particular classes or persons; other working arrangements, rules and discipline; trade union; and sympathetic action. Stoppages over wages and conditions of employment account for the majority of cases, and from data gathered in Britain it has been found that these two categories encompassed 95 per cent of cases throughout the country. This represents however, only one perspective, and on closer examination it has been found that these kinds of issues have an ambiguous status. Research by Warner and Low (1947) in the US found that most of the formal demands by strikers concerned wages and the recognition of the union, yet when they interviewed employees before and during the strike it was revealed that many of the basic grounds for discussion had little to do with such explicit causes.

Another study by Meredith (1948) also focused on the anatomy of the strike and the feature that he found extraordinary was the disparity between the precipitating causes and the amount of feeling necessary to lead to such extreme action. In this light he interpreted the issue more as a 'bone of contention' rather than the actual cause of the strike. Work along similar lines by Kelsall (1958) led him to distinguish between the logical and the psychological components of strikes.

A further piece of research bridging the gap between complaints and strikes was a longitudinal study of industrial unrest, conducted in a medium-sized chemical factory (Knowles 1965). It was found that industrial unrest occurred in a cyclical pattern so that a relatively long period of industrial quiet gave way to period of industrial unrest involving complaints and the lodging of grievances. As the situation deteriorated further, which it tended to do rapidly, it culminated in mass meetings and strikes; in such periods ' heat and mass resentment dominated the scene'. The resolution of the conflict at this stage would bring the situation back to normal, and the company would enter another period of industrial harmony and the recommencement of the cycle. The rate of labour turnover in the company also correlated with the pattern of undustrial unrest, so that employees joining the organisation during the normal periods remained with the company approximately 50 per cent longer than those joining the firm in periods of upheaval.

From the above it can be seen that industrial unrest may be regarded as the final stage of a lengthy process of deterioration: the onset of the final stages may be marked by complaints or grievances, with the climax of the deterioration being the mass meeting or strike.

In this context it can be seen that the measure of industrial unrest used in this study represented only the end-point of the process, and another method of tapping the deterioration at an earlier stage of development would have been far more helpful. Nevertheless, the general case applying to the other variables is also relevant in this instance. Again, the problem of industrial unrest in sections 'f' and 'i' can only be understood against the total background of those sections. The unrest is not a problem that will be quickly rectified. Rather it is indicative of a far wider and more general problem pervading those sections, and the treatment of the problem should lie more properly in diagnosing the predisposing factors and treating the causes of the dysfunction rather than its symptoms.

Concluding discussion

From the preliminary analysis of the relationship between the organisational variables and the behavioural factor identified in Table 3.2 it was found, as shown in Table 4.1, that labour turnover, job satisfaction of employees and work anxiety correlated significantly with this central construct typifying but distinguishing the sections. When, however, the measurement of these variables permitted their own complex structures to be identified more precisely it was possible to examine constituent components to see if any were linked with the behavioural factor already isolated. A summary of these results is presented in Table 4.10.

Table 4.10 indicates that where it was feasible to specify the components comprising these multifaceted variables the relationship between them and the central structual construct was much stronger

Table 4.10

Revised table of correlations between each variable and the factor scores of the sections on the principal component relating to the remaining set of variables

Variable	Remaining set of variables			
	r	t	df	p<
P	0.17	0.60	12	NS
Q	0.20	0.70	12	NS
C	0.33	1.24	12	NS
JSE_1	0.74	3.77	12	0.01
JSS_2	0.69	3.33	12	0.01
WA	0.58	2.49	12	0.05
Ab_1	0.64	3.01	12	0.05
LT	0.71	3.50	12	0.01

Note: JSE_1 refers to the first factor extracted in the analysis of data pertaining to the job satisfaction of employees, see Table 4.4;
JSS_2 refers to the second factor extracted from the job satisfaction of supervisors' data, see Table 4.7;
Ab_1 refers to the first factor derived from the absence analysis, see Tables 4.19 and 4.10.

than previously shown. In other words from this analysis social-psychological dimension emerged as a central construct affecting dissatisfaction, work anxiety, accidents, absence, labour turnover and industrial unrest. Frequently these are regarded as separate and distinct problems, but the empirical date in this study revealed them to be in the nature of a cluster of interrelated problems.

One of the difficulties that may tend in everyday life to obscure these relationships is the masking effect that from time to time can shroud the kinds of problems with which we are dealing. This arises from the tendency for their surface manifestations to be transformed into specific and concrete issues whereas in reality the actual problems have structural origins.

On the other hand, apart from sharing common roots as the reviews of the literature showed, these problems do not stem wholly from structural causes and many factors contribute to their determination. Nor are they affected to the same degree in this respect, and some are more sensitive than others to the quality of the internal constructs. This appeared to be particularly true for a variable such as absenteeism where factors external to the organisation contribute substantially to its formation. Nevertheless the results draw attention to the need to view the sections as social systems displaying widely varying degrees of effective functioning.

5 Towards a definition of viable and dysfunctional organisational units

In this chapter further relationships between the organisational variables are examined, and an attempt is made to identify consistent differences between the organisational units in terms of both structural and process characteristics. In addition the way in which the internal structure of these units affected both performance and satisfaction is explored.

Exceptions to the general pattern

The further this analysis has been pursued the more pervading have been the patterns identified as linking the variables examined in this study. Perhaps the stage has been reached when some of the obvious exceptions to these merging relationships should be taken into account. Earlier, reference was made to the diversity of human behaviour — its variety, variation, and variability. The literature is certainly replete with examples of inconsistent relationships between organisational variables, and these characteristics are amply illustrated in Table 2.17. Section 'f' is a case in point. Here absence was low while labour turnover was high, a situation reported previously by Kerr (1947). Conversely, in section 'h' high absence occurred with low labour turnover. Furthermore, in section 'e' high accidents went with low absence; high accidents occurred at the same time as low turnover; and so on. The present findings showed how readily these apparently paradoxical results could occur, indicating that the state of any single variable could not be comprehended in isolation but should be seen against the general pattern of all variables in any given section. The concordance relationship shown in Table 2.17 indicates a common condition underlying the variables, and illustrates visually the effect reported in the previous chapter.

Let us now take the case of section 'c' which shows that favourable attitudes did not in themselves guarantee high production. This confirmed similar findings by Brayfield and Crockett (1955), Herzberg et al. (1957), and Porter and Lawler (1968). In the case of sections 'i' and 'f' the reverse was true — high levels of production were not necessarily associated with high levels of job satisfaction, a result also reported by Kahn and Katz (1960). Although Vroom (1964) observed that surveys of the literature overall tend to reveal a positive correlation between performance and satisfaction, because of these two ways in which particular cases can run counter to the general tendency, Table 2.17 illustrates why the correlation on balance will probably always be low.

It should also be noted of sections 'i' and 'f' that production targets could be reliably met irrespective of widespread dissatisfaction, high labour turnover, and general industrial unrest. These reuslts illustrate how authoritarian leadership which traditionally is production oriented can be regarded as being successful where production is the main result valued by an organisation. It also bespeaks the difficulty confronting personnel specialists if asked to demonstrate how their programmes aimed at increasing job satisfaction and labour stability will raise production when, evidently, this can be attained without either of the former factors being present.

One of the implications of Table 2.17 is that as production levels could only be obtained by incurring considerable expenses measured in terms of poor quality and high costs of production, it is gravely misleading and organisationally dangerous if performance is defined narrowly in terms of production only. It is important to include aspects of both quality and cost effectiveness in any measure of performance and to use this broader criterion if technical effectiveness is to be realistically portrayed. Furthermore, apart from the more visible expenses involving quality and costs of production there are the less apparent costs associated with dissatisfaction, labour turnover and industrial unrest. Hence if precision in the measurement of cost effectiveness were increased the overall correlation between performance and attitudes may be higher yet again.

Viable and dysfunctional units

With some of the latter stipulations uppermost in mind the sections were re-examined so that emphasis could be placed upon two considerations. Firstly, there was the need to base assessment upon performance, i.e. not upon production only but also upon quality and costs. Secondly, weight needed to be given to the practical desirability of achieving balanced performance, a principle long recognised in classical management theory (Urwick 1943)). In other words the next step was to rate sections favourably if performance was satisfactory on all all three measures simultaneously, and penalise them for unfavourable performance on one or more of its independent measures. This was accomplished by rating the sections on a four point scale according to whether performance with respect to production, quality and costs was very satisfactory, satisfactory, unsatisfactory, or very unsatisfactory. These categories were designated respectively as ++, +, -, --, and this enabled the profile shown in Table 5.1 to be constructed.

This procedure permitted an overall ranking of performance to be obtained. When this was compared with the ranking of the sections on their behavioural structure the two were found to be positively correlated ($r = 0.57$, $p < 0.05$ with 12 df).

Table 5.1 indicates that the achievement of balanced performance

Table 5.1

Comparison of sections ranked on performance and social structure

Organisational dimension	Section													
	a	g	j	m	d	b	k	n	h	e	i	l	f	c
Production	++	++	+	–	+	+	––	+	–	–	++	––	+	––
Quality	+	+	+	++	–	++	++	+	––	––	––	––	––	––
Costs	++	++	++	+	+	–	+	––	–	––	––	+	––	––
Ranking (performance)	1.5	1.5	3	4	5	6.5	6.5	8	9.5	9.5	11	12.5	12.5	14
Ranking (social structure)	4	2	3	9	6	11	10	1	5	8	14	13	12	7

and the maintenance of sound behavioural structure were mutually consistent goals. This relationship has two important implications. Firstly, if behavioural structure is allowed to deteriorate the chances of achieving balanced performance become increasingly remote. Conversely, if balanced performance is forsaken and undue emphasis is given to the attainment of only one of the performance objectives, sooner or later deleterious effects affecting dissatisfaction of either or both employees and supervisors are bound to arise, and endemic problems involving accidents, absence, labour turnover or industrial unrest seem certain to develop.

Following this reformulation of our definition of performance the relationship between the organisational variables can now be finally shown in Table 5.2.

It is now possible to identify one of the central findings of this research: the distinction that can be made between viable and dysfunctional organisational units. The viable units may be defined as those capable of satisfactory performance over a range of technical goals; organisationally the units are stable, and members tend to derive satisfaction from this type of working environment. It is interesting to note that where morale is high, as it would be in these kinds of situations, members tend to express widespread confidence — in themselves, in their colleagues and in their leadership (Mahoney 1956, Moday, Porter and Dubin 1974).

With the dysfunctional units the opposite pattern of results tends to exist: the units are incapable of balanced achievement, and satisfactory performance tends to be restricted to only a narrow range of goals; dissatisfaction tends to be widespread; and the units are unstable, as measured by indexes including accidents, absence, labour turnover and industrial unrest. Under these conditions low levels of confidence can be expected to prevail — people are likely to lack confidence in their leadership, in their colleagues, and in themselves.

Behavioural interdependence

Put in this context it can now be seen that any single variable will always be intimately linked with a number of other variables occurring within a given situation. This property can be considered from two complementary points of view — one dealing with the structural connections between the variables, the other taking and treating the activities or processes associated with the variables. Each approach

Table 5.2

Table of correlations between each variable and the central
behavioural construct

Variable	Remaining set of variables			
	r	t	df	$p <$
Pe	0.54	2.17	12	0.05
JSE_1	0.74	3.77	12	0.01
JSS_2	0.69	3.33	12	0.01
WA	0.58	2.49	12	0.05
Ab_1	0.64	3.01	12	0.05
LT	0.71	3.50	12	0.01

Note: Pe refers to overall or balanced performance. The correlation
entered here is slightly lower than the earlier one appearing
in Table 5.1 since, in the present calculation, Pe was correlated with the behavioural construct, in keeping with the
practice adopted in Table 4.10.

can now be pursued a little further.

Structural aspects

While Table 5.2 is useful in quantifying the relationships between the organisational variables it is also helpful to represent graphically the way these variables are structurally interconnected as shown in Figure 5.1. This figure shows that the emerging structure linking the variables, although complex, is amenable to a more simple and ordered representation, and reveals a web of associations linking all the variables on which we have empirical data.

It is to be stressed that a number of the constructs shown here, especially the more familiar ones, can be expected to occur elsewhere, if not everywhere. They are probably universal, except that their ubiquity would undoubtedly mean that the strength of the relationships found on different occassions would vary from time to time and place to place depedning upon local circumstances. On the other hand other constructs (e.g. Ab_2, JSS_4) may be idiosyncratic and peculiar to the particular conditions prevailing at the site of the current study. Thus any replication of the study may lead to the disappearance of the esoteric constructs altogether, or alternatively they may be shown to be modifications of more widely applicable constructs temporarily unrecognisable.

Process aspects

The present study was designed essentially from a structural point of view and little thought was given to the possibility that process issues would arise. Nevertheless they did, and at this stage it was helpful for a number of these characteristics to be taken into account.[1]

For instance the high turnover experienced in section 'f' meant that relatively high levels of inexpereinced labour would have had to be recruited, which in turn would have adversely affected the quality of production. Once a section was in this position further processes would operate to work against measures taken to rectify the situation. For example in section 'i' the planning of production schedules and the allocation of personnel to specific tasks would have been thwarted by absenteeism. In addition the frequent emergency reallocation of personnel would keep the section under continuous production pressure, which would tend not only to decrease its ability to meet desired qualtiy standards but more importantly to

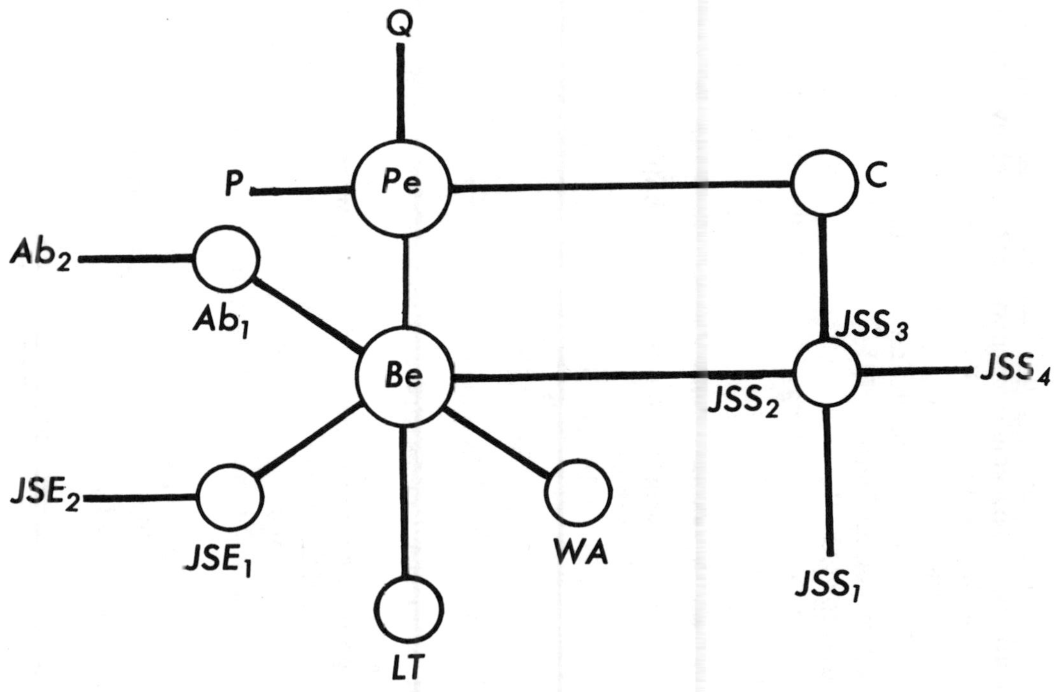

Figure 5.1 Relationships bonding performance and behavioural structure

lead to the development of resistant attitudes; these in turn would make for higher levels of absenteeism.

Research and clinical experience have shown how people accomodate to these kinds of stressful situations. Normally the employee adapts by utilising certain defences. He may rationalise by saying that the problems are too difficult to solve, he may daydream, or become apathetic. The employee may seek relief by temporarily retreating or withdrawing from the situation through absence or accidents, or he may adopt psychological attitudes in which concrete or materialistic factors assume greater importance than less tangible interpersonal or human factors. Alternatively, he may develop hostile attitudes towards the organisation, blame management when things go wrong or channel energy and creativity into deliberate acts of sabotage. In this way the employee works out the hostility through inferior quality, restriction of output, or laxity regarding costs or expenses. Not unnaturally management may react to these circumstances by harassing the employee, or by implementing tighter controls, particularly through the harsher exercise of authority — reactions which again are bound to compound the situation. Under these conditions the need to escape mounts even higher, and although it was beyond the scope of the research to identify in detail the adaptive processes employed in particular cases, Table 2.17 is useful in illustrating how withdrawal became used increasingly as an accomodating mechanism as organisational deterioration progressively increased.

For the group of more viable sections the processes would have operated in a similar manner but in the opposite direction, so that beneficial factors would tend to facilitate each other's functioning, and organisational units once working satisfactorily would tend to recreate conditions conducive to effective functioning. Thus, in keeping with this property of interdependence the relationships shown in Figure 5.1 illustrate how situations once established tend to be self-reinforcing and self-perpetuating.

Internal structure: a unifying construct

In the search for internal structure in this study the results revealed that it was possible to progress from the characteristic of cross-sectional consistency reported earlier in the research to this more diffuse property of behavioural interdependence which highlights the necessary and essential interrelationships between one variable and its family of related variables. Although the research design ensured

that this construct would emerge essentially as a structural phenomenon the differences in organisational processes occurring between
the sections showed that similar conclusions could also be reached by
taking a fundamentally different perspective. In other words structure and process are alternative way of examining the same phenomenon This is reminiscent of Argyris' (1954) proposition that there
is no essential difference between structure and process. Drawing
upon the work of biologists, he put it this way: that organisational
structures are organisational processes viewed in a static state, while
organisational processes refer to organisational structures viewed in
a dynamic state.

While it is apparent that there is an interface at which there is no
clear distinction between structure and process, by the same token
it can also be stated that neither the performance nor the behavioural
variables shown in Figure 5.1 can be effectively separated. This
suggests that in the final analysis no meaningful distinction can be
drawn between whole or part, structure or process, or performance
and behavioural elements. By way of example this can be illustrated
in Figure 5.2 where, in simplified form, the performance and behavioural components of this highly integrated and unified construct
have been represented. Figure 5.2 also shows that all system outputs
are constituted in varying degrees by both components, and all can
be considered to be a manifestation of this central construct. For
these reasons, rather than simply using a bland term such as internal
structure to signify this construct, it may be more meaningful to
identify it as organisational culture, or something similar which will
denote its diffuse and systemic properties.[2]

It is also apparent that the internal construct identified in this
manner corresponds with a number of other concepts that occur in
the literature. For example there is a close correspondence between
the construct and what Homans (1950) described as the organisation's internal system — the pattern of activities, interactions and
sentiments which arise partly out of the organisation's external
system, and partly on account of elements within the situation, as in
the Bank Wiring Observation Room. In turn, this relates closely to the
informal organisation, as previously discussed (Chapter 1). Alternatively, Brown (1960) distinguished between the 'manifest' and the
'extant' organisation, with the manifest situation corresponding to
what is normally called the formal organisation, and the extant organisation describing the situation as it really exists. Similarly Litterer
(1965) drew a distinction between the theoretical and the actual

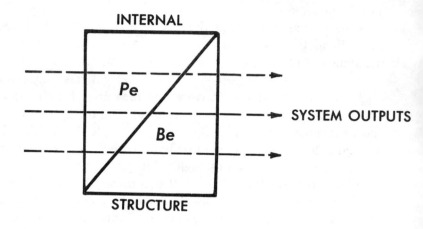

Figure 5.2 Schematic representation of the composition of internal structure.

Note: diagram illustrates that all organisational effects have both performance and behavioural components.

102

organisation to exemplify the difference between the organisation as it is supposed to be and as it is in reality. No attempt will be made here to develop a case for advocating one approach over another. Each serves different purposes and gives information and insights which are probably impossible to derive from the other perspectives.

Intensification

While the preceding analysis has identified some of the features of this systemic property operating with the organisational units, the influence which internal structure exerts upon the criterion variables needs to be examined more specifically. To take labour turnover as an example, research has shown it to be sensitive to changing economic conditions (Woytinski 1942, Cook 1951, Behrend 1953). Over the period of the study economic conditions were stable, and contributed to the divisional turnover rate of 58.8 per cent per annum. Within the division, however, as has been previously pointed out, turnover between the sections ranged from 0.0 to 105.4 per cent per annum, showing that internal factors exercised a substantial effect upon this variable. Similarly, wide differences have already been reported between the sections regarding levels of job satisfaction of employees, yet the sample and its composition were chosen because the jobs were comparable both in terms of type of work and the level of skill employed. Again, internal factors played a key role in determining satisfaction at work.

Not dissimilar results were obtained by Lawler et al. (1974) when they examined organisational climate and its relationship to organisational structure, process and performance. In this study it was found that the relationship between formal structure (hierarchy, line/staff position, sub-unit size, etc.) and performance was low ($r = 0.15$), as was the relationship between formal process variables (e.g. performance review, professional autonomy) and job satisfaction ($r = 0.09$). The relationships between these elements and organisational climate were generally higher ($r = 0.12$ and 0.34 respectively), and higher still between climate and both performance and job satisfaction ($r = 0.25$ and 0.47 respectively). It was concluded that organisational climate should be regarded as an intervening variable operating between the causal and the end-result variables.

At this stage it is impossible to state what relationship exists between internal structure and organisational climate (e.g. Sells,

1963; Forehand and Gilmer, 1964; Halpin and Crofts, 1963; Margulies, 1965; Bass, 1967; and Friedlander and Margulies, 1969).

Presumably climate is one facet of the wider social/psychological construct identified in the current research. On the other hand the present data covering a broader range of criterion variables perhaps established more sharply the role played by an organisation's internal structure: it appears to act as an intervening construct exercising an intensification effect on those aspects of formal structure and formal process which influence performance and satisfaction. Earlier figures may now be modified, as shown in Figure 5.3, to illustrate more clearly the effect of internal structure in influencing system output variables.

These results have important implications for management's role since previously emphasis has been placed upon management establishing an appropriate formal structure and developing effective specialist and administrative processes, whereas the present findings indicate that influences emanating from these sources will only be effective if a satisfactory internal structure is also developed within the organisation.

Conclusions

(1) Distinctions were drawn between viable and dysfunctional organisational units. Viable units were those capable of satisfactory performance over a range of technical goals; organisationally the units were stable, and members tended to derive satisfaction from this type of working environment.

(2) In the dysfunctional units the opposite pattern of results existed: the units were incapable of balanced achievement, and satisfactory performance tended to be restricted to a narrow range of goals; dissatisfaction tended to be widespread; and the units were unstable, as measured by indexes including accidents, absence, labour turnover and industrial unrest.

(3) All variables tended to reflect this pervasive condition in the organisational units, and although wide variations could occur in particular instances, the behaviour of any single variable could only be understood by relating it to the general pattern affecting the remaining variables.

(4) In addition to the far-ranging structural differences between the units there were also consistent differences in organisational

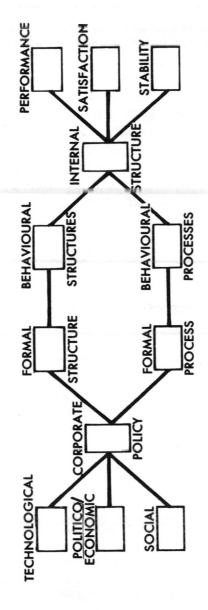

Figure 5.3 Exchanges and reciprocations between the organisation and its environment.

PERFORMANCE

SATISFACTION

STABILITY

INTERNAL STRUCTURE

BEHAVIOURAL STRUCTURES

BEHAVIOURAL PROCESSES

FORMAL STRUCTURE

FORMAL PROCESS

CORPORATE POLICY

TECHNOLOGICAL

POLITICO/ ECONOMIC

SOCIAL

processes. One of the most noticeable of these concerned the observation that withdrawal became increasingly used as an accommodating mechanism as structural deterioration within the organisational units progressively increased.

(5) Since structure and process appeared to be lternative ways of looking at the same phenomenon it could be interpreted that the two shared a common interface and formed a binding and unifying construct distinguishing between the viable and dysfunctional organisational units.

(6) There was also some evidence to suggest that this was not a passive but an active construct intervening in the way the causal variables in this company affected the system output variables. The internal structure prevailing in the viable organisational units appeared to facilitate the achievement of high performance and satisfaction, and to have the opposite effect in the dysfunctional units. This property was termed intensification.

Notes

1   The condition and sequences of events described here were reported by the supervisors during the period of data collection and analysis, see note 1, Chapter 2.
2   I am grateful to Professor E.H. Schein of MIT who suggested the use of the term culture to denote the construct described here.

6 General conclusions and implications

In this chapter the main findings of our analysis of organisational functioning are summarised. The discussion aims to highlight the major conclusions of the study and draw attention to the connection between the results and other properties of social systems either identified in allied research or recognised from clinical or practical experience. From a theoretical point of view systems theory would favour this form of extrapolation — from the organisational units analysed here to division, departments, even total organisations — but since some of the points suggested are made inferentially it will remain for further research to confirm or deny these expectations and generalisations.

A convenient starting point in discussing the study's main findings and implications is to draw attention to the fact that performance has structural origins. This could not be said for the individual aspects of performance — in this case production, quality, costs — or at least the relationships taken singly were much weaker. When a premium was placed upon balanced achievement between the three measures structural effects were more evident.

One important implication of this result is that performance requirements need to be carefully established. 'Productivity' is a good example, for in the literature this has come under many guises — particularly as a simple measure of output. The current results, however, demonstrated that dysfunctional organisational units were just as capable as viable units in meeting output or production targets. The extant situation was only realised when information about the inferior quality and the excessive costs of manufacture in the dysfunctional units became available. Consequently not only should the dimensions of performance in any given situation be clearly specified but managerially the organisation's information system would have to be developed to such a degree that knowledge of results would be available in all areas where quick corrective action was important in rectifying sub-standard performance.

In general terms, then, the results imply that in economies where demand is high management could afford, and in an instrumental sense might even be wise, to pay less attention to issues not explicitly connected with the volume of production. On the other hand in more market oriented economies, or in an economic climate of price sensitive competition, the significance of broadly defined and balanced performance requirements would have to assume greater significance.

Again it was shown that all the social/psychological indexes analysed in this study shared common roots. At one level this was a suprising result in so far as all these variables at least manifestly represent different problems. For example, by definition one would expect that job satisfaction would be largely determined by factors inherent in the job, although more recently it has been shown that people from different socio-economic backgrounds tend to expect and derive different levels of satisfaction from work, indicating that satisfaction can be influenced to some degree by societal factors. In the present company only the supervisors' levels of satisfaction depended primarily upon task oriented conditions, and even then the prevailing behavioural structure of the organisational units was an important determinant of satisfaction at work. More significantly at the employee level it was the prevailing behavioural structure of the organisational units which was a principal determinant of satisfaction at work.

Similar conclusions can be reached with respect to the other social/psychological variables. Thus, in contrast to their multiple, external sources of determination, one of the main thrusts of the research was to illustrate the importance of the structural origins of problems associated with these variables. As a corollary the results also indicate that structural problems call for structural solutions. This principle would apply to programmes of accident prevention, curtailment of industrial unrest, and reduction of absenteeism or labour turnover. Similarly, these findings may explain why some programmes of job enrichment have been disappointing, for the current results indicate that if substantive gains in satisfaction are to be attained programmes should aim not only at restructuring the job but also at changing the behavioural structure of the organisational setting in which the person works. Obviously satisfaction will marginally increase if itemised sources of dissatisfaction are removed, or partial improvements can be gained with respect to particular personnel statistics, such as absence or labour turnover, but substantive improvements will necessitate changes of a more fundamental and structural order.

A central discovery in the research was the underlying structure linking performance and the social/psychological variables. Despite its complexity this structure could be represented graphically so that the way these variables were bonded could be clearly illustrated. In practice this would mean that we can expect to begin an investigation by examining a given organisational problem: low productivity, dissatisfaction, absenteeism, or the like. Our analysis, however, should lead us to another, and then another facet of the problem, until we realise we have encountered not a single issue but a series of interelated ones. The effect is systemic: properties of a part are dependent upon properties of the whole, and vice versa.

This characteristic can be exemplified in the distinction that can be made between viable and dysfunctional work organisations. Viable work organisations can be expected to be capable of satisfactory performance over a range of technical goals — in other words, the more viable the organisation the richer and more diverse should be its performance capabilities. Organisationally the units can be expected to be stable, with people tending to derive satisfaction from this type of working environment. These work organisations can be expected to exude confidence — people will have confidence in their own capabilities and achievements and in the contributions of both their fellow workers or colleagues and their leaders.

With dysfunctional work organisations the opposite pattern of results can be expected: the units will be incapable of balanced achievement, and satisfactory performance will tend to be restricted to a narrow range of goals; dissatisfaction will tend to be widespread, and people will operate under high levels of stress and anxiety; and the units will be unstable, as measured by indexes including accidents, absence, labour turnover and industrial unrest. Under these conditions low levels of confidence can be expected to prevail — people are likely to lack confidence in their leadership, in their colleagues, and in themselves. Here high levels of hostility and aggression should abound, and in these situations, raked and rent by internecine strife, differences of interest or temperament are likely to be exacerbated into personality clashes.

Low levels of participation, involvement and commitment can be expected as part of the behavioural syndrome. For example instead of delaying the effects of minor illness until the weekend, a pattern characteristic of viable work organisation, absence from work may be delayed from the weekend until the start of the working week. It has been shown that leave of absence due to accidents can also be situationally caused, especially with employees who do not want to leave their place of employment permanently, so in dysfunctional work situations it can be expected that there will be a higher incidence of staff seeking temporary relief through this form of short term absence from work. In this way carelessness, and occasionally recklessness, can be built into the situation as accommodating mechanisms. Alternatively, the situation may foster the development of attitudes of learned helplessness.

Organisationally this wrecks havoc with managerial practices. Absence upsets the planning of work schedules of supervisors who consequently tend to wait for, and react to, circumstances, rather than plan ahead in order to prevent them. Labour turnover dilutes the skills available in the work force, so that the supervisor again is heavily committed to showing new employees elementary aspects of the job. More importantly there is an erosion of the mutual support, cohesion and teamwork that characterises the viable work organisation. These factors, of course, take their toll on performance and under increasingly difficult circumstances the situation will tend to stabilise at a level at which the work organisation is capable of only fundamental performance requirements. To prevent the complete collapse of morale expectations are lowered so that people produce the barest minimum they believe will be accepted by the organisation.

Ironically, working environments create their own contagious effects which are stimulating and uplifting with respect to performance and satisfaction as far as viable work organisations are concerned, but depressing, debilitating and enervating if the work organisation is dysfunctional. Thus, factors within these situations tend to compound upon each other intensifying the effects already present and creating a state of affairs which is self reinforcing and self perpetuating. On account of the intricate and elaborate network of structures and processes on the one hand, and the accentuating forces operating within each context on the other, it can be seen that situations once established will be resistant to change. For this reason any programme of planned change must achieve an alteration in the behavioural foundation of any work organisation if it is to have lasting effects. If this cannot be reasonably ensured then like so many examples in this field the situation is bound to revert to its original form once the novelty of the intevention has been dissipated (Seashore and Bowers 1970).

This is not to suggest that the design of formal structure is unimportant. Certainly it is, as discussed in Chapter 1. But while an inadequate structure can make high performance and satisfaction difficult to achieve,attention to formal structure alone will not guarantee that the desired effects will be forthcoming. This has been demonstrated in the work of Turner, Roberts and Roberts (1977), who showed that the employment of specialist labour relations staff, and the development of active joint consultation and formal conciliation procedures, may actually increase conflict betwen management and unions, increase the incidence of stoppages, and reduce managerial efficiency.

The present research suggests that if alterations to formal structure are to be effective then at the same time changes to the behavioural basis of management must also occur. These may come about through team-building, the improvement of intergroup relations (Beckhard 1969), process consultation (Schein 1969), management education (Hunt 1966), or a host of other approaches, but the point of the present study is that unless the process is pursued long enough

112

and far enough the dangers of reversion or regression will remain imminent. The function of this research is not to prescribe the kinds of techniques or methods available; rather it is to indicate the dimensions of the changes that are essential if the programme is to be at all successful.[1]

While this research shows that under natural conditions wide differences of the kind characterising viable and dysfunctional work organisations can be expected to occur, it can also be said that it is too risky to let the organisation's internal structure establish itself purely by chance. The proper development of a viable internal structure will require sound planning. With new organisations this should occur at the outset, at the architectural and engineering phase, so that the physical working environment is determined with the needs of the people who are to operate it fully in mind. For organisations that are going concerns company policy and practice must ensure the maintenance of the organisation as a viable social system, with adequate consideration also given to its regeneration and revitalisation.

By way of a post script a final comment may be made about organisational forms: farm or factory, shop or section, office or laboratory, classroom or committee, crew or team, gang or squad, family, or indeed any social system characterised by large numbers of variables which to some degree, or at one time or another, appear to be unknown, unrelated and uncontrollable. In these smaller systems, and indeed in larger social systems such as societies or civilisations, similar results to those described in the present account may well be expected, and if so they should have similar implications for the technical, financial or political management of these entities.

Notes

1   One of the difficulties in this area is to judge just how effective these programmes are. A major problem is that any form of organisational change is difficult to assess. Armenakis and Feild (1975) have drawn attention to the limitations of using non-independent measures to assess gains claimed from change programmes, and have pointed out that because of the financial orientation of business enterprises some measures are bound to show improvements over time irrespective of any organisational intervention. As discussed previously the importance of developing adequate measures of performance is

of paramount importance if the benefits of organisational change are to be gauged with any degree of confidence.

Appendix 1

Formal organisation chart

DIVISIONAL
MANAGER

Section	Product Manager A				Product Manager B						Product Manager C			
	a	b	c	d	e	f	g	h	i	j	k	l	m	n
Number of employees	6	29	21	26	19	21	22	11	55	22	15	22	34	11

Appendix 2

Format of the weekly expenditure report

This report dealt with four major aspects of costs which themselves constituted a number of separate items.
The four major aspects were:
* direct labour
* direct labour losses
* hourly paid indirect labour
* overtime and nightshift premiums

Direct labour

This was the total expenditure on productive operations throughout the cost centre in a single week. It included all labour clearly related and conveniently traceable to specific parts, such as the labour of machine operators and assemblers. Viewed in another way, it included pay to operatives working under incentives as well as pay for operatives on 'production time' for which no incentive scheme was appropraite.
Direct labour was constituted by four major items:
* standard direct labour
* rate variance
* operational variance
* production time variance

Standard direct labour

Every operation performed in the production process was given a standard time, usually established MTM (Method Time Measurement) or some similar technique. These operations were also evaluated at a standard rate of pay, and this rate was constant from one cost revision to the next. By this means each job was appraised as taking a specific time to complete, and carried a certain rate of pay. The standard direct labour gave the value of the work performed and provided a measure of actual production.

Rate variance

This was the difference in the rate of pay between the job evaluation rate and the rate actually paid. The additional expense was incurred when it was necessary to use more highly skilled operatives

116

than those normally required for the job. The total rate variance was the difference between the standard rate per hour and the actual rate per hour, multiplied by the actual number of hours involved.

Operational variance

The difference between the time actually spent on the job and the estimated time that the job should have taken was called operational variance. It was calculated by taking the difference between actual hours and standard hours, and pricing this at the standard rate of pay. This could also be called 'wage' variance.

Production time variance

For some productive jobs no standards were available, and the standard cost had to be estimated. Production time variance was the difference between the estimated time and the straight time taken to do the job.

Direct labour losses

Under this heading were all amounts paid to direct workers for activities of a non-productive nature. Items included here were:
* repairs
* set-up by incentive workers
* materials handling by direct workers
* cycle allowance or machine limitation
* waiting, idle, and down time
* guarantee or GMU (Guaranteed Minimum Unit)
* 15 per cent time work premium
* subsidy-measured
* subsidy-unmeasured
* training or retraining of operators
* all other direct labour losses

Repairs

These costs were those involved in making good work which had been incorrectly performed. Example of these repairs included: missed operations which had already been paid for, redrilling or reaming holes made incorrectly, filling holes bored in wrong places and drilling new holes in the correct places, touching up damaged paintwork, reshaping of parts of prevent fouling at the assembly stage, and altering parts that were outside tolerance.

Set-up by incentive workers

This referred to set-up work done by direct workers as distinct from that done by hourly paid indirect setters or by setter/operators.

Materials handling by direct workers

Sometimes incentive workers were required to do work other than the specific operations pertaining to the manufacture of parts. Work normally done by bogey-men was classified under this heading. This type of work was done when the operator would otherwise have been on waiting time.

Cycle allowance or machine limitation

Payment was made here when one or more machines operating within a group of machines was out of production. This could have been due to bad grouping, machine breakdown, or failure to keep all the machines within the group supplied with work.

Waiting, idle and down time

Operatives booked onto waiting time when they could not be engaged on productive work. This occurred with machine breakdown, or through lack of materials where it was impossible to reallocate work for them or to transfer them temporarily to another department.

Guarantee or GMU

When an operator could not sustain a rate of work called a 60 unit-hour, payments were made to bring his pay up to this guaranteed minimum unit. As training should have enabled every operator to reach this standard these payments should not have been constantly reoccurring.

15 per cent time work premiums

This was a subsidy paid to people on time-work where there was no opportunity for incentive payments.

Subsidy-measured

Payments of this kind were made as additions to standard cost and could have been brought about by temporary production problems.

Subsidy-unmeasured

These payments were also at a unit-hour higher than normal. As they could not be measured by industrial engineering, they were subjective in nature.

Training or retraining of operators

All payments on the learner scale were shown against this item. As the operator developed and his rate of production increased, the standard labour value of his production was transferred to standard direct labour so that only the balance remained under this heading.

All other direct labour losses

These were payments made to operators who otherwise would have been on waiting time. It included jobs such as cleaning floors and other odd jobs.

Hourly paid indirect labour

Into this category fell the wages of people who, although they did not perform the specific operations by which parts were manufactured, yet provided support necessary for production activities generally. Such people were paid by the hour and included setters, inspectors, labourers, etc.

Overtime and nightshift premiums

Overtime and nightshift, introduced so that production targets would be met, were paid at a higher rate, for example at time and a half or double time depending upon the period worked. These additions to costs were shown separately. Thus, if employees worked at time and a half only the half was shown in this category, and the time was shown against indirect labour. Alternatively, if direct labour was involved it was separated into direct labour and direct labour losses.

Appendix 3

Description of each of the ten job aspects
constituting the questionnaire for supervisors

Aspects of the Job	Description
Communication (Com)	Aspects of the job involving the spread of information in any direction within the organisation
Company (Coy)	Includes what the supervisor thinks of the company, and what he thinks is senior management's feeling towards him
Physical Working Conditions (PWC)	Physical aspects of the work place which are not necessarily a part of the work
Security (Se)	Features of the job which lead to assurance of continual employment, either with the same company or within the same type of work
Social Aspects of the Job (So)	The relationship of the supervisor with other members of the work group, and other supervisors
Management (Mgt)	The relationship of the supervisor with his manager
Wages (W)	The total amount of earnings
Work Ease (WE)	Aspects associated with the level of difficulty of the job
Work Interest (WI)	Interest in the job, and sense of pride in accomplishment given by the job
Work Variety (WV)	The variety of tasks available in the job

Appendix 4

Sample table showing categories of accident cases causing fatality

Type of category	% of cases
Vehicles and mobile machinery	40
Falling or moving objects, objects being handled	22
Falls between levels	11
Machinery	6
Electricity	5
Burns and explosives	5
Striking against fixed objects	2

Bibliography

Ackoff, R.L., 'Systems, organisations and interdisciplinary research', *General Systems*, vol. 5, 1960, pp. 1—8

Acton Society Trust, *Size and morale*, Acton Society Trust, London 1953

Aldridge, J.F.L., 'Emotional illness and the working environment', *Ergonomics*, vol. 13, 1970, pp. 613—21

Argyle, M., Gardner, G. and Cioffi, F., 'Supervisory methods related to productivity, absenteeism and labour turnover,' *Human Relations*, vol. 11, 1958, pp. 23—40

Argyris, C., *Organisation of a bank*, Labour and Management Centre, Yale University, New Haven 1954

Armenakis, A.A. and Field, H.S., 'Evaluation of organisational change using nonindependent criterion measures', *Personnel Psychology*, vol. 28, 1975, pp. 39—44

Bakke, E.W., 'The human resources function', in E.W. Bakke et al. (eds.), *Unions, management and the public*, Harcourt, Brace, New York 1960

Barnard, C., *The functions of the executive,* Harvard University Press, Cambridge, Mass. 1938

Bass, B.M., 'Social behaviour and the inventory theory: a review', *Psychological Bulletin*, vol. 68, 1967, pp. 260—92

Baumgartel, H. and Sobol, R., 'Background and organisation factors in absenteeism', *Personnel Psychology*, vol. 12, 1959, pp. 431—43

Beckhard, R., *Organisation development: strategies and models*, Addison-Wesley, Reading, Mass. 1969

Behrend, H., 'Absence and labour turnover in a changing economic climate', *Occupational Psychology*, vol. 27, 1953, pp. 69-79

Behrend, H., 'Voluntary absence from work', *International Labour Review*, Vol. 79, 1959, pp. 109-40

Blau, P.M. *Dynamics of bureaucracy*, University of Chicago Press, Chicago 1955

Bordow, A., 'The job satisfaction of lecturing staff at Colleges of Advanced Education', *Australian Psychologist*, vol. 9, 1974, pp. 174-83

Boyd, J.B., 'Interests of engineers related to turnover, selection and management' *Journal of Applied Psychology*, vol. 45, 1961, pp. 143— 9

Brayfield, A.H. and Crockett, W.H., 'Employee attitudes and employee performance', *Psychological Bulletin*, vol. 52, 1955, pp. 396—24

Brissenden, P.F. and Frankel, F., *Labour turnover in industry*, Macmillan, New York 1922

Brown, C.W. and Ghiselli, E.E., 'Prediction of labour turnover by aptitude tests', *Journal of Applied Psychology*, vol. 37, 1953, pp. 9—12

Brown, W., *Explorations in management*, Penguin, Harmondsworth, Middx. 1960

Buck, V., *Working under pressure*, Stapies, London 1972

Burns, T. and Stalker, G., *The management of innovation*, Barnes and Noble, Social Science Paperbacks, New York 1961

Cameron, C.E., 'Job satisfaction of employees in a light engineering firm: a case study', *Personnel Practice Bulletin*, vol. 26, 1970, pp. 34—41

Child, D., *The essentials of factor analysis*, Holt, Rinehart & Winston, London 1970

Chadwick-Jones, J. K., 'The social psychology of absenteeism', paper presented to International Congress of Applied Psychology, Munich 1978

Cleland, D.I. and King, W.R., *Systems analysis and project management*, McGraw-Hill, New York 1968

Cobb, S. and Rose, R.M., 'Hypertension, peptic ulcer and diabetes in air traffic controllers', *Journal of the American Medical Association*, vol. 224, 1973, pp. 489—92

Coch, L. and French, J. Jnr., 'Overcoming resistance to change', *Human Relations*, vol. 1, 1948, pp. 512-32

Cook, P.H., 'Labour turnover research', *Personnel Management*, vol. 33, 1951, pp. 2—9

Cooper, C.L.K. and Marshall, J., 'Occupational sources of stress: a review of the literature relating to coronary heart disease and mental ill health', *Journal of Occupational Psychology*, vol. 49, 1976, pp. 11—28

Cooper, R. and Foster, M., 'Sociotechnical systems' *American Psychologist*, vol. 26, 1971, pp. 467—74

Crowther, J., 'Absence and turnover in the divisions of one company, 1950—1955', *Occupational Psychology*, vol. 31, 1957, pp. 256—65

Crozier, M., *Bureaucratic phenomena*, University of Chicago Press, Chicago 1964

Dalton, M., *Men who manage*, Wiley, New York 1959

Davis, R.C., *The fundamentals of top management*, Harper & Row, New York 1951

Dohrenwend, B.S. and Dohrenwend, B.P., *Stressful life events*, Wiley, New York 1974

Drake, C.A., 'Accident-proneness: a hypothesis', *Character and Persons*, vol. 8, 1940, pp. 335-41

Drucker, P.F., *The practice of management*, Harper & Row, New York 1954

Emery, F.E. and Trist, E.L., 'The causal texture of organisational environments', *Human Relations*, vol. 18, 1963, pp. 20–6

Fayol, H., *General and industrial management*, Dunod, Paris 1916 (trans. Pitman, London 1949)

Felton, J.S. and Cole, B., 'The high cost of heart disease', *Circulation*, vol. 27, 1963, pp. 957–62

Finn, F., Hickey, N. and O'Doherty, E.F., 'The psychological profiles of male and female patients with CHD', *Irish Journal of Medical Science*, vol. 2, 1969, pp. 339-41

Fisher, B., *Determining the costs of labour turnover*, US Bureau of Labour Statistics, Bulletin 227, 1917

Fisher, V.E. and Hanna, J.V., *The dissatisfied worker*, Macmillan New York 1931

Fleishman, E.A. and Harris, E.F., 'Patterns of leadership behaviour related to employee grievance and turnover', *Personnel Psychology*, vol. 15, 1962, pp. 43-56

Follet, M.P., in H. Metcalf and L. Urwick (eds.), *Dynamic administration*, Harper & Row, New York 1942

Forehand, G.A. and Gilmer, B. von Haller, 'Environmental variation in studies of organisational behaviour', *Psychological Bulletin*, vol. 62, 1964, pp. 361–82

Fox, J.B. and Scott, J.F., *Absenteeism: management's problem*, Harvard Business Research Studies no. 29, Harvard University Press, Cambridge, Mass. 1943

Fraser, R., *The incidence of neurosis among factory workers*, Medical Research Council, Industrial Health Research Board No. 90, London 1947

French, W., 'Processes vis-à-vis systems', *Journal of the Academy of Management*, vol. 6, 1963, pp. 46-57

Friedlander, F. and Margulies, N., 'Multiple impacts of organisational climate and individual value systems upon job satisfactions', *Personnel Psychology*, vol. 22, 1969, pp. 171–83

Galbraith, J., *Designing complex organisations*, Addison-Wesley, Reading, Mass. 1973

Gaudet, F.J., *Labour turnover: calculation and cost*, American Management Association, New York, Research Study 39, 1957

Ghiselli, E. E. *The validity of occupational aptitude tests*, Wiley, New York 1953

Gouldner, A.W., *Patterns of industrial bureaucracy*, The Free Press, Glencoe, Ill. 1954

Graicunas, V.A., 'Relationships in organisations'. in L. Gulick and L. F. Urwick (eds.), *Papers on the science of administration*, Institute of Public Administration, New York 1937

Guion, R.M., 'A note on organisational climate', *Organisational Behaviour and Human Performance*, vol. 9, 1973, pp. 120–5

Gulick, L. and Urwick, L.F., *Papers on the science of administration*, Institute of Public Administration, Columbia University, New York 1937

Hage, J. and Aiken, M., 'Routine technology, social structure and organisational goals', *Administrative Science Quarterly*, Vol. 14, 1969, pp. 366–77

Haire, M., 'Biological models and empirical histories of the growth of organisations', M. Haire (ed.), *Modern organisation theory*, Wiley, New York 1959

Hakkinen, S. and Toivainen, Y., 'Psychological factors causing labour turnover among underground workers', *Occupational Psychology*, vol. 34, 1960, pp. 15–30

Halpin, A. W. and Crofts, D. E., *The organisational climate of schools*, University of Chicago Press, Chicago 1963

Harvey, E., 'Technology and the structure of organisations', *American Sociological Review*, vol. 33, 1968, pp. 247–59

Henrici, S.B., *Standard costs for manufacturing*, McGraw-Hill, New York 1960

Herbst, P.G., 'Measurement of behavioural structures by means of input–output data', *Human Relations*, vol. 19, 1957, pp. 335–45

Herbst, P.G., *Autonomous group functioning*, Tavistock, London 1962

Herman, J.B. and Hulin, C.L., 'Managerial satisfaction and organisational roles: an investigation of Porter's need deficiency scales', *Journal of Applied Psychology*, vol. 57, 1973, pp. 118–24

Herzberg, F., Mausner, B., Peterson, R.O. and Capwell, D.F., *Job attitudes: review of research and opinion*. Psychological Services of Pittsburgh, Pittsburg 1957

Hickson, D.J., Pugh, D.S. and Pheysey, D.C., 'Operations technology and organisational structure: an empirical reappraisal, *Administrative Science Quarterly*, vol. 14, 1969, pp. 378–97

Hill, J.M.M., 'A consideration of labour turnover as the resultant of a quasi-stationary process', *Human Relations*, vol. 4, 1951, pp. 255–64

Hill, J.M.M. and Trist, E.L., 'A consideration of industrial accidents as a measure of withdrawal from the work situation', *Human Relations*, vol. 6, 1953, pp. 357–80

Homans, G.C., *The human group*, Harcourt, Brace & World, New York 1950

Hoppock, R., *Job satisfaction*, Harper, New York 1935

Horngren, C.T., *Cost accounting: a management emphasis*, Prentice-Hall, Englewood Cliffs, NJ 1967

Hulin, C.L., 'Effects of community characteristics on measures of job satisfaction', *Journal of Applied Psychology*, vol. 50, 1966, pp. 185–92

Hulin, C.L. and Blood, M.R., 'Job enlargement, individual differences, and worker responses', *Psychological Bulletin*, vol. 69, 1968, pp. 41–55

Hunt, N.C., 'The universities' place', in N.C. Hunt and T.S. Milne (eds.) *Modern thinking in management*, Clark, Edinburgh 1966

Huse, E.F. and Taylor, E.K. 'Reliability of absence measures', *Journal of Applied Psychology*, vol. 46, 1962, pp. 159–60

Indik, B.P., 'Some effects of organisation size on member attitudes and behaviour', *Human Relations*, vol. 16, 1963, pp. 369–84

Isambert-Jamati, V., 'Absenteeism among women workers in industry', *International Labour Review*, vol. 85, 1962, pp. 248–61

Jaques, E., 'Studies in the social development of an industrial community (the Glacier projects),' *Human Relations*, vol. 3, 1950, pp. 223–49

Jaques, E., *The changing culture of a factory*, Tavistock, London 1951

Jenkins, C.D., 'Psychological and social precursors of coronary disease', *New England Journal of Medicine*, vol. 284, 1971, pp. 244–55

Kahn, R.L. and Katz, D., 'Leadership practices in relation to productivity and morale', in D. Cartwright and A. Zander (eds.), *Group dynamics: research and theory*, Tavistock Publications, London 1960

Kahne, H.R., Ryder, C.M., Snegriff, L.S. and Wyshak, G., 'Don't take older workers for granted', *Harvard Business Review*, vol. 35, 1957, pp. 90–4

Kaiser, H.F., 'Comments on communalities and the number of factors' presented on 14 May at an informal conference: the communality problem in factor analysis, Washington University, St Louis 1960

Katz, D. and Kahn, R.L., *The social psychology of organisations*, Wiley, New York 1966

Katz, D., Maccoby, N. and Morse, Nancy, C., *Productivity, supervision and morale in an office situation*, University of Michigan, Institute for Social Research, Ann Arbor, Mich. 1950

Katz, D., Maccoby, Gurin, E. and Floor, L. G., *Productivity, supervision and morale among railroad workers*, University of Michigan, Institute for Social Research, Ann Arbor, Mich. 1951

Keenan, T., Kerr, W.A. and Sherman, W., 'Psychological climate and accidents in an automotive plant', *Journal of Applied Psychology*, vol. 35, 1951, pp. 108–11.

Kerr, W.A., 'Labour turnover and its correlates', *Applied Psychology*, Vol. 31, 1947, pp. 366–71

Kerr, W.A., 'Accident proneness of factory departments' *Journal of Applied Psychology*, vol. 34, 1950, pp. 167–70

Kerr, W.A., 'Complementary theories of safety psychology', *Journal of Social Psychology*, vol. 45, 1957, pp. 3–9

Kerr, W.A., 'Complementary theories of safety psychology', *Journal of Social Psychology*, vol. 45, 1957, pp 3–9

Kerr, W.A., Koppelmeier, G.J., and Sullivan, J.J., 'Absenteeism, turnover and morale in a metals fabrication factory', *Occupational Psychology*, vol. 25, 1951, pp. 50–5

Klein, V., *Working wives*, Institute of Personnel Management, London, Occasional Papers, no. 4, 1961

Knowles, M.C., 'A longitudinal study of labour turnover', *Personnel Practice Bulletin*, vol. 20, 1964, pp. 25–37

Knowles, M.C., 'A review of labour turnover research', *Personnel Practice Bulletin*, vol. 21, no. 2, 1965, pp. 6–17

Knowles, M.C., 'The nature of industrial accidents', *Journal of Industrial Relations*. vol. 14, 1972, pp. 125–31

Knowles, M. C., 'Industrial relations in Australia: an organisational perspective', *Journal of Industrial Relations*, vol. 16, 1974, pp. 21–8

Knowles, M.C., 'Interdependence among organisational variables', *Human Relations*, vol. 28, 1975, pp. 431–50

Knowles, M. C., 'Labour turnover: aspects of its significance', *Journal of Industrial Relations*, vol. 18, 1976, pp. 67–76

Knowles, M. C., 'Organisationally induced absenteeism', *Journal of*

Industrial Relations, vol. 21, 1979, pp. 351—357.

Knowles, M. C. and Knowles, A. D., 'Factors affecting job satisfaction of supervisors', *Journal of Industrial Relations*, vol. 20, 1978, pp. 138—45

Knowles, M. C and Knowles, A. D., 'job satisfaction and the organisation's internal structure', *Australian Journal of Management*, vol. 4, 1979, pp. 69—78

Kornhauser, A.W., 'The study of work feelings', *Personnel Journal*, vol. 8, 1930, pp. 348—51

Kuriloff, A.H., 'An experiment in management — putting theory Y to the test', *Personnel*, vol. 40, 1963, pp. 9—17

Lahiri, D.K. and Srivastva, S., 'Determinants of job satisfaction in middle-management personnel', *Journal of Applied Psychology*, vol. 51, 1967, pp. 254—65

Lawler, E.E. III, Hall, D.T. and Oldham, G.R., 'Organisational climate: relationship to organisational structure, process and performance', *Organisational Behaviour and Human Performance*, vol. 11, 1974, pp. 139—55

Lawrence, P. and Lorsch, J., *Organisation and environment: managing differentiation and integration.* Harvard University Graduate School of Business Administration, Division of Research, Boston 1967

Levinson, H., 'Management by whose objectives', *Harvard Business Review*, July-August 1970, pp. 125—34

Liddell, F.D.K., 'Attendance in the coal-mining industry', *Britsh Journal of Sociology*, vol. 5, 1954, pp. 78—86

Likert, R., *New patterns of management*, McGraw-Hill, New York 1961

Likert, R., *The human organisation*, McGraw-Hill, New York 1967

Litterer, J.A., *The analysis of organisations*, Wiley, New York 1965

Lodahl, T.M., 'Patterns of job attitudes in two assembly technologies', *Administrative Science Quarterly*, vol. 8, 1964, pp. 483—519

Long, J.R., *Labour turnover under full employment*, University of Birmingham Studies in Economics and Society, Monograph A2, Birmingham, 1951

Mackenzie, R., *Personal communication*, 1966

McCarney, M.P., 'Plant level relationships: the shop steward', *Journal of Industrial Relations*, vol. 14, 1972, pp. 272—81

McGregor, D., *The human side of enterprise*, McGraw-Hill, New York 1960

Mahoney, G.M., 'Unidimensional scales for the measurement of morale in an industrial situation', *Human Relations*, vol. 9, 1956, pp. 3—26

Mahoney, G.M. and Frost, P.J., 'The role of technology in models of organisational effectiveness', *Organisational Behaviour and Human Performance*, vol. 11, 1974, pp. 122—38

Mann, F. C. and Baumgartel, H., *Absence and employee attitudes in an electric power company*, Institute for Social Research, Universirty of Michigan, Ann Arbor 1952

March, J.E. and Simon, H.A., *Organisations*, Wiley, New York 1958

Marcson, S., *Automation, alienation and anomie,* Harper & Row, New York 1970

Margolis, B.L., Kroes, W.H. and Quinn, R.P., 'Job stress: an unlisted occupational hazard', *Journal of Occupational Medicine*, vol. 16, 1974, pp. 654—61

Margulies, N., 'A study of orgnisational culture and self-actualising process', unpublished PhD thesis, University of California 1965 (cited)

Mayo, E., *The social problems of an industrial civilisation*, Harvard University Graduate School of Business Administration, Cambridge, Mass. 1945

Mayo, E. and Lombard, G., *Teamwork and labour turnover in the aircraft industry of Southern California*, Harvard University Graduate School of Business Administration, Cambridge, Mass. 1944

Meredith, J., 'The psychological aspect of strikes', *Penguin Parade*, Second Series, vol. 2, no. 43, 1948 (cited)

Merton, R.K., 'Bureaucratic structure and personality', *Social Forces*, vol. 18, 1940, pp. 560—8

Miller, J.C., 'Towards a general theory for the behavioural sciences', *American Psychologist*, vol. 10, 1955, pp. 513—31

Mintz, A. and Blum, M.L., 'A re-examination of the accident proneness concept', *Journal of Applied Psychology*, vol. 33, 1949 pp. 195—211

Monie, P., 'Job satisfaction of female employees in the clothing industry: case study no. 3', *Personnel Practice Bulletin*, vol. 23, 1967 pp. 16—26

Mooney, J., *Principles of organisation*, Harper, New York 1947

Mosel, J.N. and Wade, R.R., 'A weighted application blank for reduction of turnover in department store sales clerks', *Personnel Psychology*, vol. 4, 1951, pp. 177—84

Moth, L.G., 'Industrial relations in the plant — a study of evolution within the system', *Journal of Industrial Relations*, vol. 14, 1972, pp. 282—93

Mountain, A.D., 'Job satisfaction of female employees in the clothing industry: case study No. 1', *Personnel Practice Bulletin*, vol. 21, no. 4, 1965, pp. 7—17

Moday, R.T., Porter, L.W. and Dubin, R., 'Unit performance, situational factors and employee attitudes in spatially separated work units'. *Organisational Behaviour and Human Performance*, vol. 12, 1974, pp. 231—48

Myers, M.S., *Every employee a manager*, McGraw-Hill, New York, 1970

O'Brien, R.D., 'Job satisfaction of female employees in the clothing industry: case study No. 2', *Personnel Practice Bulletin*, vol. 22, 1966, pp. 39—46

Osborne, E.E. and Vernon, H.M., *The influence of temperature and other conditions on the frequency of industrial accidents*, Industrial Fatigue Research Board, Report no. 19, 1922

Owens, A.C., 'Sick leave among railwaymen threatened by redundancy: a pilot study', *Occupational Psychology*, vol. 13, 1966, pp. 349—60

Pahl, J.M. and Pahl, R.E., *Managers and their wives*, Allen Lane, London 1971

Patchen, M., 'Absence and employee feelings about fair treatment', *Personnel Psychology*, vol. 13, 1960, pp. 349—60

Payne, R.L., Fineman, S. and Wall, T. D., 'Organisational climate and job satisfaction: a conceptual synthesis', *Organisational Behaviour and Human Performance*, vol. 16, 1976, pp. 45—62

Pettman, B.O., 'Some factors influencing labour turnover: a review of research literature', *Industrial Relations*, vol. 4, 1973, pp. 43—61

Pigors, P. and Myers, C.A., *Personnel administration*, McGraw-Hill, New York 1956

Porter, L.W., 'A study of perceived need satisfaction in bottom and middle management jobs', *Journal of Applied Psychology*, vol. 45, 1961, pp. 1—10

Porter, L.W., 'Job attitudes in management: I. Perceived deficiencies in need fulfillment as a function of job level', *Journal of Applied Psychology*, vol. 46, 1962, pp. 375—84

Porter, L.W., 'Job attitudes in management: II. Perceived importance of needs as a function of job level', *Journal of Applied Psychology*, vol. 47, 1963, pp. 141—8 (a)

Porter, L.W., 'Job attitudes in management: III. Perceived deficiencies in need fulfillment as a function of line versus staff type of job', *Journal of Applied Psychology*, vol. 47, 1963, pp. 267–75 (b)

Porter, L.W., 'Job attitudes in management: IV. Perceived deficiencies in need fulfillment as a function of size of company', *Journal of Applied Psychology*, vol. 47, 1963, pp. 387–397 (c)

Porter, L.W. and Lawler, E.E., 'Properties of organisational structure in relation to job attitudes and job behaviour', *Psychological Bulletin*, vol.64, 1965, pp. 23–51

Porter, L.W. and Lawler, E.E., *Managerial attitudes and performance*, Irwin, Homewood, Ill. 1968

Porter, L.W. and Steers, R.M., 'Organisational, work and personal factors in turnover and absenteeism', *Psychological Bulletin*, vol. 80, 1973, pp. 151–76

Pritchard, R.D. and Karasick, B.W., 'The effect of organisational climate on managerial job performance and job satisfaction', *Organisational Behaviour and Human Performance*, vol. 9, 1973, pp. 126–46

Pugh, D.S., Hickson, D.J., Hinings, C.R. and Turner, C., 'Dimensions of organisation structure', *Administrative Science Quarterly*, vol. 13, 1968, pp. 65–105

Quinn, R.P., Seashore, S.K. and Mangione, I., *Survey of working conditions*, US Government Printing Office, Washing, DC 1971

Raphael, W., Hearnshaw, Mead, R.T., and Fraser, J.H.M., 'Report on an inquiry into labour turnover in the London district', *Occupational Psychology*, vol. 12, 1938 (cited)

Revans, R.W., 'Human relations, management and size', in E.M. Hugh-Jones (ed.), *Human relations and modern management*, North Holland, Amsterdam 1958

Rice, A.K., 'An examination of the boundaries of part-institutions', *Human Relations*, vol. 4, 1951, pp. 393–400

Rice, A.K., 'The relative independence of sub-institutions as illustrated by departmental labour turnover', *Human Relations*, vol. 5, 1952, pp. 83–90

Rice, A.K., 'The enterprise and its environment',Tavistock, London 1963

Rice, A.K., Hill, J.M.M. and Trist, E.L., 'The representation of labour turnover as a social process', *Human Relations*, vol. 3, 1950, pp. 349–72

Rice, A.K. and Trist, E.L., 'Institutional and sub-institutional determinants of change in labour turnover', *Human Relations, vol. 5,* 1952, pp. 347–71

Roethlisberger, F.L. and Dickson, W.J., *Management and the worker* Harvard University Press, Cambridge, Mass. 1939

Roy, D.F., 'Efficiency and the fix: informal intergroup relations in a piece-work machineshop', *American Journal of Sociology*, vol. 60, 1954, pp. 255–66

Roy, D.F., '"Banana-time": job satisfaction and informal interaction', *Human Organisation*, vol. 18, 1960, pp. 158–68

Ryder, Leonie, A., 'Job satisfaction of female employees in the clothing industry: case study No. 5,' *Personnel Practice Bulletin,* vol. 25, 1969, pp. 309–20

Schein, E.H., *Organisational psychology,* Prentice-Hall, Englewood Cliffs, NJ 1965

Schein, E.H., *Process consultation*, Addison-Wesley, Reading, Mass. 1969

Schultz, J.R., 'Blueprint for executive joh satsifaction', *Personnel,* vol. 41, 1964, pp. 8–18

Seashore, S.E., 'Criteria of organisational effectiveness', in *'Assessing organisational performance with behavioural measurements,* Foundation for Research on Human Behaviour, Ann Arbour, Mich. 1964

Seashore, S.E. and Bowers. D.G., 'Durability of organisational change', *American Psychologist,* vol. 25, 1970, pp. 227–32

Sells, S.B. (ed.), *Stimulus determinants of behaviour,* Ronald Press, New York 1963

Selznick, P., 'An approach to a theory of bureaucracy', *American Sociological Review,* 1943 (cited)

Shephard, J.M., *Automation and alienation*, MIT Press, Cambridge, Mass. 1971

Shepherd, R.D. and Walker, J., 'Absence from work in relation to wage level and family responsibility', *British Journal of Industrial Medicine,* vol. 15, 1958, pp. 53–9

Silverman, D., *The theory of organisations,* Heinemann, London 1970

Simon, H.A. 'The architecture of complexity', *Proceedings of the American Philosophical Society*, vol. 106, 1962, pp. 467–82

Stone, E. F. and Porter, L. W., 'Job characteristics and job attitudes: a multivariate study', *Journal of Applied Psychology,* vol. 60, 1975, pp. 57–64

Strong, E.K. Jr., *Vocational interest of men and women*, Standard University Press, Stanford 1943

Talacchi, S., 'Organisational size, individual attitudes and behaviour: an empirical study', *Administrative Science Quarterly, vol. 5, 1960,* pp. 398–420

Thompson, J.D., *Organisations in action*, McGraw-Hill, New York 1967

Tiffin, J., *Industrial psychology*, Allen & Unwin, London 1951

Tredgold, R.F., 'Insecurity in industry', *Proceedings of the Royal Society of Medicine*, vol. 65, 1972, pp. 1087–9

Trist, E.L. and Bamforth, K.W., 'Some social and psychological consequences of the longwall method of coal-getting', *Human Relations*, vol. 4, 1951, pp. 3–38

Trist, E.L., Higgin, G.W., Murray, H. and Pollock, A.E., *Organisational choice*, Tavistock Publications, London 1963

Turner, A.K. and Lawrence, P.R., *Industrial jobs and the workers: an investigation of response to task attributes*, Harvard University Graduate School of Business Administration, 1965

Turner, H. A., Roberts, G. and Roberts, D., *Management characteristics and labour conflict*, Cambridge University Press, Cambridge 1977

Twenty Personnel Executives, 'The function and scope of personnel administration', *Personnel,* vol. 24, 1947, pp. 5–8

Urwick L.F., *The elements of administration*, Harper, New York 1944

Van Beck, H.G., 'The influence of assembly line organisation on output, quality and morale', *Occupational Psychology,* vol. 38, 1964, pp.161–72

Vaughan, E. G. and Gardner, G., 'Technology as an explanatory variable in the study of worker attitudes', *Journal of Industrial Relations*, vol. 18, 1976, pp. 99–111

Veil, C., *L'absentéisme*, Report Presente aux journees de la Sante Mentale, Paris, 1960 (cited)

Vernon, H.M., *Accidents and their prevention*, Macmillan, New York 1937

Viteles, M.S., 'Selection of cashiers and predicting length of service', *Journal of Personnel Research,* vol. 2, 1924, pp. 467–73

von Bertalanffy, L., 'An outline of general systems theory', *British Journal of Philosophical Science,* vol. 1, 1950, pp. 134–65

von Bertalanffy, L., 'General systems theory', *General Systems,* vol. 1, 1956, pp. 1–10

Vroom, V., *Work and motivation*, Wiley, New York 1964

Walker, C.R. and Guest, R.H., *The man on the assembly line*, Harvard University Press, Cambridge, Mass. 1952

Walker, K.F., 'Conflict and mutual misunderstanding: a survey of union leaders' and business executives' attitudes', *Journal of Industrial Relations*, vol. 1, 1959, pp. 20–30

Walker, K.F. and Lumsden, J., 'Employees' job satisfaction and attitudes – a survey', *Business Review*, March, 1963, pp. 20–4

Warner, W.L. and Low, J.O., *The social system of the modern factory: the strike – a social analysis*, Yale University Press, New Haven, Conn. 1947

Warr, P.B. and Routledge, T., 'An opinion scale for the study of managers' job satisfaction', *Occupational Psychology*, vol. 43, 1969, pp. 95–109

Waters, L.K. and Roach, D., 'Relationship between job attitudes and two forms of withdrawal from the work situation', *Journal of Applied Psychology*, vol. 55, 1971, pp. 92–4

Waters, L.K. and Roach, D., 'Job attitudes as predictors of termination and absenteeism: consistency over time and across organisational units', *Journal of Applied Psychology*, vol. 57, 1973, pp. 341–2

Weber, M., *The theory of social and economic organisation, 1921, A.M. Anderson and Talcott Parsons (trans)*, Oxford University Press, New York 1947

Whitehead, A.N., *Science and the modern world*, Macmillan, New York 1925

Whyte, W.F. *Human relations in the restaurant industry*, McGraw-Hill, New York 1948

Whyte, W.F., 'The grievance procedure and plant society', in *The grievance process*, Labour and Industrial Relations Centre, Michigan State University 1956

Wickert, F.R., 'Turnover and employees' fellings of ego-involvement in the day-to-day operations of a company', *Personnel Psychology*, vol. 4, 1951, pp. 185–98

Woodward, J., *Industrial organisation*, Oxford University Press, Oxford 1965

Worthy, J.C., 'Organisational structure and employee morale', *American Sociological Review, vol. 15, 1950, pp. 169–79*

Woytinski, *W.S., Three aspects of labour dynamics*. Committee on Social Secrutiy, Social Science Research Council, Washington 1942

Subject index

Abilities, 5
Absence, absenteeism, 13, 17, 22, 36–41, 44–47, 50–52, 61, 73, 77, 82, 84, 87–89, 93, 96, 98, 104, 110–111
Accidents, 22, 35, 36, 49, 73, 81, 84–85, 93
Administrative theory, 4–6
Attitudes, 5–6, 8, 54, 67–74, 93–4, 100
Authority, 4–6, 22, 100

Bank Wiring Observation Room, 101
Behavioural activities, 5
  characteristics, 6
  construct, 56–89
  elements, 6
  structure, 50–89, 94, 109
  variables, 100–101
Budget, 25–27
Bureaucracy, 5

Centralisation, 4, 68
Chain of command, 4
Communication, 6, 13, 27, 54, 67, 73, 81, 85
  networks, 5
  patterns, 11
Company, 22, 27
Composite work organisation, 8, 13, 85
Construct, 56, 61, 87, 96–106
Control, 4–5, 25, 76, 100

Costs, 22, 25–27, 43–47, 56, 70–74, 94–95, 100, 109
Conventional work organisation, 13
Cross-sectional consistency, 45, 100

Decentralisation, 4, 68
Decision-making, 6
Departmentalisation, 5
Deterioration, 81–86, 100
Differentiation, 6
Dissatisfaction, 75–94, 104, 110–112
Durham coal-fields, 13
Duty(ies), 11–13
  statements, 5
Dysfunctional units, 75, 87, 93–114

Economic factors, 11, 83
  conditions, 21, 36, 40, 80, 103
Effectiveness, 11
Efficiency, 4
Employees, 24, 63–70, 75, 85
Environment, 8, 11, 22

Factor analysis, 51
  principal components analysis, 51–55, 67–75, 77–80
Field, 8
  field theory, 55
Finance, 5

135

Formal elements, 6
    formalisation, 5
    formal structure, 4, 6, 103, 112–113
Function, 5, 6, 68–69
    of personnel management, 55–57

Goals, 10, 55, 94
Grievance(s), 17, 41–42, 85–87
    complaints, 85–87
Group behaviour, 6, 21
    decision-making, 5–6
    growth, 5–6
    inter-group competition, 5–6
    inter-group co-operation, 5–6
    interpersonal interactions, 11
    interpersonal relations, 5, 8–9, 55
    life, 55
    norms, 5–6
    problem-solving, 5–6

Health, 77
    mental, 75–77
    neurotic illness, 13, 75
    occupational, 32
    psychosomatic symptoms, 32
    sickness, 80
Hierarchy, 11, 68–69, 103
Hostility, 40, 100, 111
Human assets, 55–56
    organization, 55–56
    resources, 6, 24, 55–56

Industrial relations, 40, 112
    department,
    unrest, 23, 40–49, 73, 85–94, 104–111
Intensification, 103–106, 112
Interdependence, 96, 100

Job, 68–69, 76, 103, 109
    characteristics, 37, 65
    conditions, 36
    enrichment, 110
    factors, 83
Job satisfaction, 6, 21, 24, 52, 88, 110–111
    of employees, 22, 27–31, 43–46, 52, 63–70, 87–89
    of supervisors, 22, 32–36, 43–46, 52, 70–74, 88–89

Labour turnover, 13, 17, 22, 37, 42, 55–56, 61, 73, 76, 81–89, 93–111
    length of service, 24, 55, 68, 83, 85
Leadership, 5–6, 17, 68, 96, 111
Legal entity, 4
Line management, 54
    and staff, 5, 68, 103
Location, 22–24

Management, 8, 22, 27, 29, 54, 56, 67, 78, 83, 100, 104, 111–115
    education, 112
Marketing, 5
Matrix, 4, 22, 49, 53, 70, 77
Measurement, 24
Model, 11
Morale, 4, 17, 55, 83, 96
Motivation, 5, 6

Objectivies, 11, 52, 56, 92
Operations, 5, 6
Organisation, 54–55, 101–104, 113
    chart, 5
    extant, 101
    informal, 101

Author index

Fraser, J. H. M., 46
Fraser, R., 75
French, W., 5
Friedlander, F., 104
Frost, P. J., 6

Gardner, G., 17, 68
Gaudet, F. J., 36, 80
Ghiselli, E. E., 46, 68
Gilmer, B. H., 55, 104
Gouldner, A. W., 5
Graicunas, V. A., 5
Guest, R. H., 6
Guion, R. M., 55
Gulick, L., 5

Hage, J., 6
Haire, M., 8
Halpin, A. W., 104
Hakkinen, S., 46
Hanna, J. V., 46, 68
Harris, E. F., 17, 46
Harvey, E., 6
Hearnshaw, R. T., 47
Henrici, S. B., 26
Herbst, P.G., 6, 17
Herman, J. B., 68, 69
Herzberg, F., 67, 93
Hickey, N., 76
Hickson, D. J., 5, 6
Higgin, G. W., 8
Hill, J. M. M. 35, 55, 56, 84
Hinings, C. R., 5
Homans, G. C., 101
Hoppoch, R., 67
Horngren, C. T., 27
Hulin, C. L., 46, 68
Hunt, N. C., 112
Huse, E. F., 36

Indik, B. P., 6

Isambert-Jamati, V., 80

Jaques, E., 55
Jenkins, C. D., 76

Kahn, R. L., 5, 8, 93
Kahne, H. R., 46, 80
Kaider, H. F., 49
Karasick, B. W., 55
Katz, D., 5, 8, 93
Keenan, T., 84
Kelsall, E. P., 86
Kerr, W. A., 36, 80, 83, 84, 85, 93
King, W. R., 5
Klein, V., 46
Knowles, M. C., 37, 46, 88, 86
Koppelmeier, G. J., 38, 80
Kornhauser, A. W., 67
Kroes, W. H., 76

Lahiri, D. K., 68
Lawler, E. E., 68, 93, 103
Lawrence, P. R. 6, 8, 18
Levinson, H., 54
Liddell, F. D. K., 46, 80
Likert, R., 17, 54
Litterer, J. A., 5, 101
Lodahl, T. M., 6
Lombard, G., 17, 46
Long, J. R., 46
Lorsch, J., 6, 8
Low, J. O., 86
Lumsden, J., 27, 46

Mackenzie, R., 54
McGregor, D., 54
Mahoney, G. M., 6, 96
Mann, F. C., 81
Mangione, I., 76
Marcson, S., 76

140